The Art Of Living Long; A New And Improved English Version Of The Treatise By The Celebrated Venetian Centenarian, Louis Cornaro, With Essays

Cornaro, Luigi, 1475-1566, Addison, Joseph, 1672-1719, Bacon, Francis, 1561-1626

LOUIS CORNARO
1464 — 1566

From the painting by Tintoretto   No. 83, Pitti Palace Gallery

Photographed by Alinari Brothers, Florence

The Art of
LIVING LONG

A NEW AND IMPROVED ENGLISH VERSION
OF THE TREATISE OF THE

CELEBRATED VENETIAN CENTENARIAN

LOUIS CORNARO

WITH ESSAYS BY
JOSEPH ADDISON, LORD BACON, AND SIR WILLIAM TEMPLE

Here is everything advantageous to life.
    —"THE TEMPEST"

MILWAUKEE
WILLIAM F. BUTLER
1903

PREFACE

Against diseases known, the strongest fence
Is the defensive virtue, abstinence.
                    —Benjamin Franklin.

FOR a people of whom less than a two-hundredth part of one per cent. reach an age that Nature intends all should pass,* the words of the aged author of "The Temperate Life" possess a deep import. To them this volume is addressed

Louis Cornaro's own account—written toward the close of more than a century of life—of the means of his complete restoration from an almost hopeless complication of bodily infirmities, to the happy state he continued so long to enjoy, may be said to form a life story, which, in its peculiar significance, is without a parallel in history
Not

> *"By showing conclusively and clearly*
> *·That death is a stupid blunder merely,*
> *And not a necessity of our lives,"*

but by demonstrating, in a manner most decisive, that the condition of perfect health—maintained to the full limit of life ordained by Nature—is a blessing within the power of every human being to realize, and by indicating the path by which all may attain it, did this excellent man earn his unique

* See Note A

[7]

position among the benefactors of mankind   Let us hope that our positive and practical age, ever ready to judge a proposition by its degree of usefulness, will perceive that a rule of life which effected the recovery of a dying man, and enabled him to retain entire mental and bodily vigor beyond his hundredth year, is of incontestable merit.

While there are some, who, though of the number of Cornaro's most zealous pupils, regret that he permitted wine to form a portion of his abstemious diet; yet, when his position on this question is contrasted with the prevailing custom of his country and age, his life is none the less recognized by all, as one of the most salutary examples of a truly temperate career the world has yet witnessed.

A carefully revised version of his celebrated treatise, made by able translators, is here presented   As a result of painstaking researches among ancient documents in the archives of Venice and Padua, historical matter relating to Cornaro and his family is also placed before the reader   Much of this is not to be found in any previous edition of his works, in the various languages into which they have been rendered

Of the other eminent writers whose teachings on the subject of longevity we have included in this volume, little need here be said   One of them, not many years after the famous centenarian had passed away, emphasized to the world, in the Latin tongue, the substantial advantages Cornaro had reaped from the habit of complete self-restraint to which he had accustomed himself in early manhood, and from which, for the remainder of his days, he had never deviated.   A century after Bacon, in the graceful tribute which Addison—one of the most practical philosophers of his age—pays to Cornaro, we have an introduction to the work of the illustrious Venetian that is truly worthy of his theme

Acknowledgment for valuable assistance is gratefully made to Conte Comm Filippo Grimani, LL. D , the honored Mayor of Venice; Cav. Prof Angelo Scrinzi, Ph D , Director of the Venetian Civic Museum, and Dr Ricciotti Bratti, his associate; as well as Dr. Prof. Andrea Moschetti, Director of the Civic Museum of Padua Thanks are due, also, to Dr Prof. Emilio Lovarini, of Bologna, and Signor Michele Danesi, Editor of "L'Arte," Rome, for their kind revision of the translation of "The Villas Erected by Louis Cornaro," and for their consent to its publication. To Cav Dr Enrico Ridolfi, Director of the Royal Galleries and National Museum of Florence, and to the photographers Signori Fratelli Alinari, of the same city, this work is indebted for the copy of the Tintoretto painting of Louis Cornaro. Credit is accorded, for many helpful courtesies, to Miss Ida M. Street, author of "Ruskin's Principles of Art Criticism," and Messrs Willard G Bleyer, of the University of Wisconsin, and John G Gregory, of Milwaukee

W. F. B.

Milwaukee, March, 1903.

Bosom up my counsel;
You'll find it wholesome.—William Shakespeare.

Deign, reader, to be taught,
Whate'er thy strength of body, force of thought.
—David Garrick.

Know, prudent, cautious, self-control
Is wisdom's root.
—Robert Burns.

Wouldst thou enjoy a long life, a healthy body, and
a vigorous mind, and be acquainted also with the wonder-
ful works of God, labor in the first place to bring thy
appetite to reason.—Benjamin Franklin.

There is no chance in results.—Ralph Waldo Emerson

CONTENTS

	Page
Preface	7
Introduction	
"To Louis Cornaro."—Randall	13
Addison, in "The Spectator," October 13, 1711	15
Part I	
The Life and Writings of Louis Cornaro.	25
"The Temperate Life" by Louis Cornaro	
First Discourse.	39
Second Discourse	77
Third Discourse.	91
Fourth Discourse.	103
Part II	
Selections from Lord Bacon's "History of Life and Death," etc	117
Selections from Sir William Temple's "Health and Long Life," etc	141
Appendix	
A Short History of the Cornaro Family	159
Some Account of Eminent Cornaros.	169
Gamba's Eulogy upon Louis Cornaro	179
Lovarini's "The Villas Erected by Louis Cornaro" . .	191
Notes	209
Portraits	
Louis Cornaro	4
Joseph Addison	52
Lord Bacon	102
Sir William Temple	152
The Cornaro Coat of Arms	6

If any man can convince me and bring home to me that I do not think or act aright, gladly will I change, for I search after truth, by which man never yet was harmed. But he is harmed who abideth on still in his deception and ignorance.

Do not think that what is hard for thee to master is impossible for man; but if a thing is possible and proper to man, deem it attainable by thee.

Persevere then until thou shalt have made these things thy own.

Like a mariner who has doubled the promontory, thou wilt find calm, everything stable, and a waveless bay.

—Marcus Aurelius Antoninus.

INTRODUCTION

TO LOUIS CORNARO

BY

John Witt Randall *

O thou that for an hundred years
   Didst lightly tread the ancestral hall,
Yet sawest thy brethren bathed in tears,
   Cut down ere ripe, and round thee fall,—

Well didst thou deem long life the measure
   Of long enjoyment to the wise,
To fools alone devoid of pleasure;
   Thou wouldst not die as the fool dies.

Robbed of thy titles, lands, and health,
   With man and fortune in disgrace,
In wisdom didst thou seek thy wealth,
   Thy peace in friendship to thy race.

With thine eleven grandchildren met,
   Thou couldst at will become the boy;
And, thine own sorrows to forget,
   Couldst lose thyself in others' joy,—

* See Note B

[13]

THE ART OF LIVING LONG

Couldst mount thy horse when past fourscore,
  And climb steep hills, and on dull days
Cheer the long hours with learned lore,
  Or spend thy wit on tales and plays.

In summer, thou wast friend of flowers,
  And, when the winter nights grew long,
And music cheered the evening hours,
  Still clearest was the old man's song.

Thus, while thy calm and thoughtful mind
  The ravages of time survived,
Three generations of mankind
  Dropped round thee, joyless and short-lived.

Thou sawest the flowers of youth decay,
  Half dried and withered through excess,
Till, nursed by virtue's milder ray,
  Thy green age grew to fruitfulness.

Thou sawest life's barque on troubled seas
  Long tossed; care's clouds thy skies o'ercast;
But calm content, with moderate breeze,
  Brought thee to wisdom's port at last.

Life's evening, wherein most behold
  Their season of regrets and fears,
Became for thee an age of gold,
  And gave thee all thy happiest years

As gentle airs and genial sun
  Stay winter's march when leaves grow sere,
And, when the summer's race is run,
  With a new summer crown the year,

INTRODUCTION

So temperance, like that lingering glow
Which makes the October woods so bright,
Did on thy vale of years bestow
A glorious autumn of delight.

What useful lessons might our race
From thy so sage experience draw!
Earth might become a joyous place,
Would man but reverence nature's law.

Soar folly, self, and sense above,
Govern each mutinous desire,
Nor let the sacred flame of love
In passion's hurricane expire

No wondrous works of hand or mind
Were thine; God bade thee stand and wait,
A living proof to all thy kind
That a wise man may master fate

Happy that life around whose close
The virtues all their rainbows cast,
While wisdom and the soul's repose
Make age more blest than all the past!

THERE* is a story in the "Arabian Nights' Tales" of a king who had long languished under an ill habit of body, and had taken abundance of remedies to no purpose. At length, says the fable, a physician cured him by the following method: he took a hollow ball of wood, and filled it with several

* See Note C

drugs; after which he closed it up so artificially that nothing appeared. He likewise took a mall; and, after having hollowed the handle, and that part which strikes the ball, he inclosed in them several drugs after the same manner as in the ball itself. He then ordered the sultan, who was his patient, to exercise himself early in the morning with these rightly prepared instruments, till such time as he should sweat; when, as the story goes, the virtue of the medicaments perspiring through the wood, had so good an influence on the sultan's constitution, that they cured him of an indisposition which all the compositions he had taken inwardly had not been able to remove. This Eastern allegory is finely contrived to show us how beneficial bodily labor is to health, and that exercise is the most effectual physic. I have described in my hundred and fifteenth paper, from the general structure and mechanism of a human body, how absolutely necessary exercise is for its preservation, I shall in this place recommend another great preservative of health, which in many cases produces the same effects as exercise, and may, in some measure, supply its place, where opportunities of exercise are wanting. The preservative I am speaking of is temperance; which has those particular advantages above all other means of health, that it may be practiced by all ranks and conditions, at any season or in any place. It is a kind of regimen into which every man may put himself, without interruption to business, expense of

money, or loss of time. If exercise throws off all super-
fluities, temperance prevents them; if exercise clears the
vessels, temperance neither satiates nor overstrains
them; if exercise raises proper ferments in the humors,
and promotes the circulation of the blood, temperance
gives nature her full play, and enables her to exert herself in all her force and vigor; if exercise dissipates a
growing distemper, temperance starves it.

Physic, for the most part, is nothing else but the
substitute of exercise or temperance. Medicines are
indeed absolutely necessary in acute distempers, that
cannot wait the slow operations of these two great instruments of health; but did men live in a habitual course
of exercise and temperance, there would be but little
occasion for them. Accordingly, we find that those parts
of the world are the most healthy where they subsist by
the chase; and that men lived longest when their lives
were employed in hunting, and when they had little food
besides what they caught. Blistering, cupping, bleeding,
are seldom of use but to the idle and intemperate; as all
those inward applications which are so much in practice
among us, are for the most part nothing else but expedi-
ents to make luxury consistent with health. The apothecary is perpetually employed in countermining the
cook and the vintner. It is said of Diogenes, that, meeting a young man who was going to a feast, he took him
up in the street and carried him home to his friends, as
one who was running into imminent danger, had not he

prevented him. What would that philosopher have said, had he been present at the gluttony of a modern meal? Would not he have thought the master of a family mad, and have begged his servants to tie down his hands, had he seen him devour fowl, fish, and flesh; swallow oil and vinegar, wines and spices; throw down salads of twenty different herbs, sauces of a hundred ingredients, confections and fruits of numberless sweets and flavors? What unnatural motions and counter-ferments must such a medley of intemperance produce in the body! For my part, when I behold a fashionable table set out in all its magnificence, I fancy that I see gouts and dropsies, fevers and lethargies, with other innumerable distempers, lying in ambuscade among the dishes.

Nature delights in the most plain and simple diet. Every animal, but man, keeps to one dish. Herbs are the food of this species, fish of that, and flesh of a third. Man falls upon everything that comes in his way; not the smallest fruit or excrescence of the earth, scarce a berry or a mushroom, can escape him.

It is impossible to lay down any determinate rule for temperance; because what is luxury in one may be temperance in another. But there are few that have lived any time in the world, who are not judges of their own constitutions, so far as to know what kinds and what proportions of food do best agree with them. Were I to consider my readers as my patients, and to prescribe such a kind of temperance as is accommodated to all persons, and such as is particularly suitable to our climate and way of living, I would copy the following rules of a very eminent physician: Make your whole repast out of one dish; if you indulge in a second, avoid drinking anything strong till you have finished your meal; at the same time abstain from all sauces, or at least such as are not the most plain and simple. A man could not be well guilty of gluttony, if he stuck to these few obvious and easy rules. In the first case, there would be no variety of tastes to solicit his palate, and occasion excess; nor, in the second, any artificial provocatives to relieve satiety, and create a false appetite. ... But, because it is impossible for one who lives in the world to diet himself always in so philosophical a manner, I think every man should have his days of abstinence, according as his constitution will permit. These are great reliefs to nature, as they qualify her for struggling with hunger and thirst, whenever any distemper or duty of life may put her upon such difficulties; and at the same time give her an opportunity of extricating herself from her oppressions, and recovering the several tones and springs of her distended vessels. Besides that, abstinence well-timed often kills a sickness in embryo, and destroys the first seeds of an indisposition. It is observed by two or three ancient authors, that Socrates, notwithstanding he lived in Athens during that great plague, which has made so much noise through all ages, and has been celebrated at different times by such eminent hands; I say, notwithstanding that he lived in the time of this devouring pestilence, he never caught the least infection; which those writers unanimously ascribe to that uninterrupted temperance which he always observed.

And here I cannot but mention an observation which I have often made, upon reading the lives of the philosophers, and comparing them with any series of kings or great men of the same number. If we consider these ancient sages, a great part of whose philosophy consisted in a temperate and abstemious course of life, one would think the life of a philosopher and the life of a man were of two different dates. For we find that the generality of these wise men were nearer a hundred than sixty years of age at the time of their respective deaths. But the most remarkable instance of the efficacy of temperance toward the procuring of long life, is what we meet with in a little book published by Louis Cornaro the Venetian; which I the rather mention, because it is of undoubted credit, as the late Venetian ambassador, who was of the same family, attested more than once in conversation, when he resided in England. Cornaro, who was the author of the little "Treatise" I am mentioning, was of an infirm constitution, till about forty; when, by obstinately persisting in an exact course of temperance, he recovered a perfect state of health; insomuch that at fourscore he published his book, which has been translated into English under the title of "A Sure and Certain Method of Attaining a Long and Healthy

Life." He lived to give a third or fourth edition of it; and, after having passed his hundredth year, died without pain or agony, and like one who falls asleep. The "Treatise" I mention has been taken notice of by several eminent authors, and is written with such a spirit of cheerfulness, religion, and good sense, as are the natural concomitants of temperance and sobriety. The mixture of the old man in it is rather a recommendation than a discredit to it.—JOSEPH ADDISON IN "THE SPECTATOR," October 13, 1711.

Of all tyrants, custom is that which to sustain itself stands most in need of the opinion which is entertained of its power, its only strength lies in that which is attributed to it. A single attempt to break the yoke soon shows us its fragility. But the chief property of custom is to contract our ideas, like our movements, within the circle it has traced for us. It governs us by the terror it inspires for any new and untried condition. It shows us the walls of the prison within which we are inclosed, as the boundary of the world, beyond that, all is undefined, confusion, chaos; it almost seems as though we should not have air to breathe.

—F. P. G. Guizot.

PART I

"THE TEMPERATE LIFE"

BY

LOUIS CORNARO

PREFACED BY A SHORT ACCOUNT OF HIS
LIFE AND WRITINGS

'Tis in ourselves that we are thus or thus Our bodies are gardens; to the which our wills are gardeners: so that if we will plant nettles or sow lettuce, set hyssop and weed up thyme, supply it with one gender of herbs or distract it with many, either to have it sterile with idleness or manured with industry, why, the power and corrigible authority of this lies in our wills. If the balance of our lives had not one scale of reason to poise another of sensuality, the blood and baseness of our natures would conduct us to most preposterous conclusions but we have reason to cool our raging motions, our carnal stings, our un-bitted lusts.—"Othello"

A Short Account of

THE LIFE AND WRITINGS

OF

LOUIS CORNARO

TO LOUIS CORNARO

FROM THE ITALIAN OF HIERONIMO GUALDO (CIRCA 1560)
DONE INTO ENGLISH VERSE BY
JOHN GOADBY GREGORY

I

Sir, well may Fame to you accord the praise
 That, spite of adverse stars and nature's strife,
 Solely by measured conduct of your life,
Healthy and happy you gained length of days.
Nor stops approval there, but also weighs
 The pains you spared not to set others right,
 Guiding their footsteps by your beacon-light
To long and pleasant journeying through life's maze.
Blest is your lot, who, with a steadfast mind,
 Beneath a load of years which many fear,
Contented and felicitous abide,

[25]

Your voice in song upraised robust and clear,
Your thoughts with noble studies occupied.
That good is yours which is for man designed.

II

"Weary and woeful is senectitude
  E'en when from penury and aches 'tis free,"
  Cries one, "for that it brings debility,
And warns us of the grisly monarch rude."
Yet he who holds in rein his passions crude,
  Nor rends the blossoms from life's growing tree,
  Gathers in age fruits sweet and fair to see,
For Nature is with purpose kind endued.
If I, now years come on, am weak and ill,
  Not time, but I, am cause of this my woe.
Too much I heeded headlong appetite.
And though to save the wreck I bend my will,
  'Tis vain, I fear—I ever older grow,
And aged error is not soon set right

III

In hermit caverns, where the desert glowers,
  The ancient Fathers lived on frugal fare—
  Roots, cresses, herbs—avoiding viands rare,
Nor had they palates less refined than ours.
From their example, confirmation flowers
  Of what you tell me, and in mind I bear
  That feasts which folly spreads on tables fair
Our frames enfeeble and reduce our powers.

The wish in man is native to remain
Long with the living, for to live is sweet.
His wish he may by abstinence attain.
Dame Reason counsels, sober and discreet,
This way that solid privilege to gain,
And tardy to the realm of shades retreat.

L OUIS CORNARO (ancient Venetian, Alvise; modern Italian, Luigi, Lodovico, or Ludovico),—often styled The Venetian Centenarian,—the author of the famous treatise, "The Temperate Life," which forms the main portion of this volume, was born in the city of Venice in the year 1464

Although a direct descendant of the illustrious family of Cornaro, yet, defrauded in some way through the dishonest intrigues of some of his relatives,—we are but imperfectly acquainted with the circumstances,—he was deprived of the honors and privileges attached to his noble birth, and excluded from all public employment in the State. A man of great personal and family pride, he felt very keenly the humiliation of this treatment, and, as a consequence, he withdrew from his native place and made the city of Padua his home for the remainder of his life, save for brief seasons of summer retirement to his country-seats.

Yet that, which, at the time, must have seemed to him a great misfortune, proved eventually a blessing, and doubtless, during the long course of his remarkable career, Cornaro's philosophic mind often reverted with thankfulness to those very indignities, but for which, perhaps, he would never have received the chief incentive of his life, for may we not believe it was because of them that he resolved to found for himself a more honorable name—one that should rest upon a sounder and more worthy basis than mere family pride. This determination, whatever may have inspired it,

[27]

proved, as we learn in his narrative, to be the crisis of his life, changing, as if by magic, its entire course, and it resulted in the establishment of a fame, not only great in his own day, but which continues to increase as time rolls on

In order to accomplish the purpose uppermost in his mind, the first thing to which he gave his constant and most intelligent attention was the securing of perfect health, which heretofore he had never known, and which he recognized as the best armor for the warfare of life, a knowledge, the importance of which—in his day, as in ours—few fully realized At the details of this glorious work, as well as its happy results, we shall here take only a hasty glance; for the picture he has painted is by the hand of a master, and no one but himself can do it justice.

Born with a very delicate constitution, accompanied unfortunately by a choleric disposition, Cornaro furthermore gave evidence, in early life, of careless habits which finally developed into those of intemperance, and, though destined to leave behind him a name imperishable, because of virtues based upon a complete subjugation of every passion, was almost destroyed, before he reached the age of forty, by those natural and acquired infirmities, which, for years, had made his days and nights an almost continual martyrdom.

Finally convinced that his unnatural habits would, if persisted in, soon be the cause of his death, and possessed of that determined courage and resolution, which, on a closer acquaintance, we shall recognize and learn to admire as his chief trait, he changed his manner of life so completely that, in a very brief time, his diseases disappeared, giving place to a rugged health and serenity of mind hitherto unknown to him In a word, from a despairing and almost helpless invalid, unfit for either work or enjoyment, he became not only a man of perfect health, singularly active and happy, but also such an example of complete self-restraint as to be the wonder and admiration of all who knew him, earning and receiving the title of The Temperate. The mildness and sweetness of his altered disposition at the same time gained for him the fullest respect and affection

In the city of Udine, northern Italy, he married Veronica di Spilimbergo,* a daughter of the noble house of that name

He very much desired children, not only for every natural reason, but also in order that his own offspring might inherit the large fortune which he possessed. Though for a long time disappointed in this hope, he was finally made very happy by the advent of a little daughter, born when he and his wife were both well advanced in years; to her they gave the name of Chiara (Clara) **   In due time she was married to one of her own name and kindred, Giovanni (John), the son of Fantino Cornaro, a member of the wealthy and powerful Cornaro Piscopia branch of the family. She became the mother of eight sons and three daughters, all of whom the grandfather—as we learn from his own words—lived to see and enjoy

Having faithfully observed that wise law of Nature, moderation, for so many years, he anticipated, with a confidence which the sequel will show was neither unfounded nor disappointed, a happy and prosperous life of not less than a century, and this span he was equally certain he would have been able to extend considerably, had it been his good fortune to have begun life with the advantages he assures us his teachings will confer on the children of all who lead the temperate life it had been his delight to follow.

To the very close of his wonderful career he retained his accustomed health and vigor, as well as the possession, in their perfection, of all his faculties   No hand but his own can faithfully give us an account of the recreations and pleasures of that happy old age for which he entreats all to strive   But we may sum it all up in the one brief line wherein he assures us: "I never knew the world was beautiful until I reached old age." Of the knowledge that his was an instance without a parallel, he himself was not ignorant   In this thought he not only took a pardonable pride, but derived one of the greatest joys of his old age, when he reflected that while many others before him had written eulogies upon a life of temperance and regularity, no one, at the end of a century of life, had ever taken pen in hand to leave to the world

* See Note D   ** See Note C

[29]

the story of a personal participation in the many indescribable blessings, which, for so many years, it had been his lot to enjoy; nor had any one, after recovering broken health, lived to such an age to tell the world how he had done so.

The one thought uppermost in his heart was that of gratitude for his recovery, and for the countless blessings of his long life. This sentiment he hoped would ever continue to bear substantial fruit, for he lived and died in the belief that his labors in writing a faithful account of his experience, would result, for all time, in benefiting those who would listen to him. He was convinced that if he, who had begun life under so many disadvantages, could attain perfect health and continue in it for so many years, the possibilities of those blessed with a perfect constitution and aided, from childhood, with the temperate rule of life, must indeed be almost unlimited. It will be difficult to find anywhere recorded an instance wherein constitutional defects, aggravated by unwise habits of life, threatened a more untimely death, and if Cornaro, with a constitution naturally weak and apparently ruined at the age of forty, could attain such results, who will presume to set a limit to the possibilities of longevity for the human family, after consecutive generations have faithfully observed Nature's wise laws?

Loaded with testimonials of the gratitude and reverence of many who had profited by his example and advice,—which knowledge of this benefit to others was, as he assures us, among the sweetest of his many blessings,—he passed the evening of his life honored by all, and in the enjoyment of the friendship and esteem of the most eminent of his countrymen Having devoted his best years to the accomplishment of what he firmly believed to be his mission in this world,—a consecrated task, that of bringing home to his fellow-men the realization of the inevitable consequences of intemperance,—he patiently waited for the end. When death came, it found him armed with the resignation of the philosopher and a steadfastly courageous faith in the future, ready and glad to resign his life Peacefully, as he had expected and foretold, he died at his palace in Padua, April

26, 1566, in the one hundred and third year of his age. (Historians have not agreed as to the year of his birth, some placing his age at one hundred and four, others as low as ninety-eight The dates we have given are, however, substantiated by the best authorities.)

He was buried on the eighth of the following month, without any pomp, according to the directions left in his will; and by his side his faithful wife, who survived him and lived to almost the same age, in due time was laid. Her end was an equally happy one, finding her in such perfect serenity of soul and ease of body, that those at her bedside were not aware that her gentle spirit had taken its flight

The beautiful home, built by Cornaro on the Via Melchiorre Cesarotti in Padua, and the scene, for so many years, of the greatest domestic happiness as well as of the most generous hospitality, is still in existence, and has always been known by his name It consists, mainly, of three buildings; the palace—which is the principal one—and the casino are both attributed to Cornaro himself; while the celebrated loggia is known as the work of his protégé and friend, Falconetto.* The three inclose a courtyard, upon which all face— the palace on one side near the street, the loggia and casino on other sides

The best portrait extant of this justly celebrated man is catalogued as No 83 in the famous gallery of the Pitti Palace, at Florence. It has, until recently, been considered one of Titian's paintings; but it is now known as the work of Tintoretto, and is among the masterpieces of that famous artist The canvas measures 44x33 inches, and the photographic copy used in this work is declared by the Director of the Pitti Gallery to be an excellent one. The figure, two-thirds in length, is life size Cornaro is represented as seated in an armchair, dressed in black, his coat trimmed with fur. Though the picture portrays a man well advanced in years, there is a dignity of bearing and a keenness of eye that indicate one still physically vigorous and mentally alert

In other portions of this volume, some of the many

* See Note E

attainments of this remarkable man are made manifest; we will here—with this passing mention of his treatise on the preservation of the lagoons ("Trattato delle Acque," Padua, 1560)—notice, very briefly, the writings for which he is chiefly known.

At the age of eighty-three, after more than forty years of perfect health and undisturbed tranquillity of spirits, during which time he had lived a life that contrasted as much with that of his earlier days as it did with that which he saw commonly lived by others around him, he wrote the first of the four discourses which constitute his famous treatise, "The Temperate Life" This was followed by the three others, one written at the age of eighty-six, one at ninety-one, and the last at ninety-five, the four completing a most instructive life story—one with which he earnestly wished all might become familiar, that they might follow his example, and thus enjoy the countless blessings which had so filled his own cup to overflowing

Centuries ago, Pythagoras, Herodicus, Hippocrates, Iccus, Celsus, and Galen—as have some in every age—waged a bitter warfare against unnatural habits of life; and accounts of the attainment of extraordinary age, both in ancient and modern times, are not uncommon. The autobiography of Cornaro, however, who, after patient search, discovered in his own person the curative and life-sustaining power of the temperate life,—and that beyond the century mark,—and who, with equal diligence, labored to impress upon others the lesson of his own experience, affords an instance without parallel in all the annals of history.

In a very brief way—more effective, he believed, than if written at greater length—does this remarkable man hand down to posterity his conviction, both from observation and experience, of the utter worthlessness of the kind of life too often seen on all sides At the same time he pictures the reward to be reaped every moment, but especially in old age, from a life spent in conformity with reason and Nature

Most particularly does he emphasize the greater value of the later years of life as compared with the earlier ones. By

the time men have acquired knowledge, judgment, and experience,—the necessary equipment of the fullest citizenship,—
they are unable, he observes, because of physical degenera-
tion, consequent on irrational and unnatural methods of living, to exercise these qualifications. Such men are then cut
off in their prime, leaving, at fifty or sixty, their life work
but half completed; and yet, as he protests, were they but to
attain extreme age as followers of the life he led, "How much
more beautiful would they make the world!"

The first edition of "The Temperate Life '—the work on
which Cornaro's fame chiefly rests—was published at Padua
in the year 1558, and few works of such small dimension have
excited wider or more fervid discussion. For three hundred
years this treatise has been a classic in his native land Translated into Latin, as also into many modern languages, it has
been popular wherever studied. Slight as the book is, it has,
and will continue to have, a permanent place in general literature; though we believe it may be questioned if many in this
country, even among the most cultured readers, have had an
opportunity of reading it.

To those only imperfectly acquainted with his story, Cornaro is merely a famous valetudinarian, who was enabled, by
temperate living, to pass the age of a hundred. Careful
readers of the book, however, will always remember him not
only as a most charming autobiographer, but also as a
man, who, having successfully solved one of life's most difficult problems, labored to encourage in others those habits
which had proved so advantageous in his own case His
assurance that, after all, this world would be a most delightful place if people would but live temperately, is the burden
of his message to mankind, and who, to-day, is ready to
declare him wrong in his assertion that man, by the weak
indulgence of his appetites, has always shortened his life and
failed to reap the countless blessings within his reach?
Convinced that from this source come most of the ills that
flesh is heir to, Cornaro writes with the confidence that those
who listen to him earnestly will not fail to heed his warning.
Thus, also, will they not only secure that perfect health of

body and mind, without which complete happiness can never be realized, but will be enabled to prolong, in honorable endeavor, that enviable condition to the extreme limit intended by Nature. He hoped that the faithful following of his counsel would transform into a universal hymn of joy the strain of despairing weariness,—so evident throughout the recorded thought of all the centuries,—in which men of all nations and ranks of life have deplored the early loss of youth and vigor, and lamented the resistless strides of premature old age.

A simple diet was almost exclusively the nourishment of the oldest peoples of Syria, Egypt, Greece, and, in their most glorious days, of the Romans, and when man shall once more take to heart this lesson of the means of enjoying uninterrupted health and full length of days,—blessings which in ages long past were almost universally enjoyed, and which man alone, and the animals under his control, now fail to possess,—the world will everywhere be blessed with the presence of those who will be considered in their prime at an age now scarcely believed attainable There will then be no doubt that life is worth living; and, because man will then seek only its true and enduring joys, those problems that for ages have distressed him will vanish of themselves—problems existing only because of the craving of the unhealthy human brain for those shadows of life so long pictured as its substance.

The reader will have spent his time in vain, however, if he fails to appreciate fully the vital importance of the fact that Cornaro's own regimen, as he most strongly insists, was intended for himself alone—that he does not urge upon everyone the extreme abstinence practiced by himself. All persons, he declares, should observe the temperate life prescribed as Nature's highest law, but, as the temperance of one man is excess in his neighbor, each must discover the suitable quantity and quality of food proper in his own individual case, and then live accordingly. It is the aim and spirit, not the letter, of his example that he implores mankind to observe.

While Cornaro's personal dietary habits are not, indeed,

applicable in detail to every individual constitution, and were never, as we have just said, intended by him as such, yet his general rules will always be correct These have had in the past, and have to-day, many followers, and the number of those who faithfully tread in the pathway indicated for them by the venerable writer, constantly enjoying, during a long and happy life, the blessings promised them, will continue to increase, let us hope, until it includes, in the not remote future, the vast majority of our race. Even in an age of wealth and luxury, such as ours, in which opportunities rapidly multiply for the gratification of every sensuous desire, we need not fear that those who choose to be critics of Cornaro and the fundamental rules of his teachings, will continue to find willing listeners. Let us hope that, in time, all will take to heart the lesson taught mankind by the bitter experience of the centuries. that the physical, moral, intellectual, and social condition now so almost hopelessly universal, is but the inevitable result of disobedience of natural law; and that man has but himself to blame when he fails to possess the greatest of earthly blessings—perfect health of body and mind—and fullness of years in which to enjoy it

Some, as thou saw'st, by violent stroke shall die,
By fire, flood, famine, by intemperance more
In meats and drinks, which on the Earth shall bring
Diseases dire, of which a monstrous crew
Before thee shall appear, that thou may'st know
What misery the inabstinence of Eve
Shall bring on men.

                If thou well observe
The rule of "Not too much," by temperance taught
In what thou eat'st and drink'st, seeking from thence
Due nourishment, not gluttonous delight,
Till many years over thy head return,
So mayst thou live, till, like ripe fruit, thou drop
Into thy mother's lap, or be with ease
Gathered, not harshly plucked, for death mature.

                    —"Paradise Lost."

"THE TEMPERATE LIFE"

BY

LOUIS CORNARO

TRANSLATED FROM THE ITALIAN OF HIS

"LA VITA SOBRIA"

IN WHICH HE DEMONSTRATES, BY HIS OWN EXAMPLE,
A SURE AND CERTAIN METHOD OF ATTAINING
A LONG AND HEALTHY LIFE

———

IN FOUR DISCOURSES

WRITTEN, SEVERALLY, AT THE AGES OF EIGHTY-THREE,
EIGHTY-SIX, NINETY-ONE, AND NINETY-FIVE

Divine Sobriety, pleasing to God, the friend of nature, the daughter of reason, the sister of virtue, the companion of temperate living, ... the loving mother of human life, the true medicine both of the soul and of the body; how much should men praise and thank thee for thy courteous gifts! for thou givest them the means of preserving life in health, that blessing than which it did not please God we should have a greater in this world—life and existence, so naturally prized, so willingly guarded by every living creature!

—Louis Cornaro.

THE FIRST DISCOURSE

WRITTEN AT THE AGE OF EIGHTY-THREE

Wherein the author details the method by which he
corrected his infirm condition, strengthened his
naturally weak constitution, and thence-
forth continued in the enjoyment
of perfect health

IT is certain that habit, in man, eventually becomes
second nature, compelling him to practice that to
which he has become accustomed, regardless of
whether such a thing be beneficial or injurious to him.
Moreover, we see in many instances—and no one can
call this into question—that the force of habit will
triumph even over reason. Indeed, if a man of good
morals frequents the company of a bad man, it very often
happens that he will change from good to bad. Yet
sometimes the contrary is equally true; namely, that
while good habits often change readily for the worse, so
also do bad habits change to good ones; since a wicked
man who has once been good may still, by frequenting
the society of the good, return to the better ways which he

had formerly followed. All these changes must be attributed solely to the force of habit, which is truly very great.

It is in consequence of this powerful force of habit, that of late, — indeed during my own lifetime and memory, — three evil customs have gradually gained a foothold in our own Italy. The first of these is adulation and ceremony, the second is heresy, and the third is intemperance These three vices, cruel monsters of human life as they truly are, have, in our day, prevailed so universally as to have impaired the sincerity of social life, the religion of the soul, and the health of the body.

Having long reflected on this unfortunate condition, I have now determined to treat of the last of these vices — intemperance, and, in order to accomplish all I can toward abolishing it, I shall prove that it is an abuse. With regard to the two other obnoxious habits, I feel certain that, ere long, some noble mind will undertake the task of condemning them and removing them from among us. Thus do I firmly hope that I shall, before I leave this world, see these three abuses conquered and crushed out of Italy, and, consequently, witness the return of my country to her wise and beautiful customs of yore.

Coming, then, to that evil concerning which I propose to speak,—the vice of intemperance,—I declare that it is a wicked thing that it should prevail to such an extent as to greatly lower, nay, almost abolish, the temperate life. For though it is well known by all that intemperance proceeds from the vice of gluttony, and temperance from the virtue of restraint, nevertheless the former is exalted as a virtuous thing and even as a mark of distinction, while temperance is stigmatized and scorned as dishonorable, and as befitting the miserly alone.

These false notions are due entirely to the force of habit, bred by men's senses and uncontrolled appetites. It is this craving to gratify the appetites which has allured and inebriated men to such a degree that, abandoning the path of virtue, they have taken to following the one of vice—a road which leads them, though they see it not, to strange and fatal chronic infirmities through which they grow prematurely old. Before they reach the age of forty their health has been completely worn out—just the reverse of what the temperate life once did for them. For this, before it was banished by the deadly habit of intemperance, invariably kept all its followers strong and healthy, even to the age of fourscore and upward.

O wretched and unhappy Italy, canst thou not see that intemperance kills every year amongst thy people as great a number as would perish during the time of a most dreadful pestilence, or by the sword or fire of many bloody wars! And these truly immoral banquets of thine, now so commonly the custom,—feasts so great and intolerable that the tables are never found large enough to accommodate the innumerable dishes set upon them, so that they must be heaped, one upon another, almost mountain high,—must we not brand them as so many destructive battles! Who could ever live amid such a multitude of disorders and excesses!

Oh, for the love of God, I conjure you to apply a remedy to this unholy condition! for I am certain there is no vice more displeasing to His Divine Majesty than this fatal one of intemperance. Let this new death, worse than any pestilence ever known, be driven out of Italy; as was the case with that other epidemic, which, though it once caused so much misery, nowadays does but very little harm,—indeed, scarcely any,—thanks to the improved state of affairs brought about by good sanitary regulations.

For there is a remedy by which we may banish this fatal vice of intemperance—an easy remedy, and one of which every man may avail himself if he will; that is, to live in accordance with the simplicity of Nature, which teaches us to be satisfied with little, to follow the ways of holy self-control and divine reason, and to accustom ourselves to eat nothing but that which is necessary to sustain life.

We should bear in mind that anything more than this will surely be followed by infirmity and death; and that while intemperance is merely a gratification of the palate,—a pleasure that vanishes in a moment,—yet, for a long time afterward, it causes the body much suffering and damage, and finally destroys it together with the soul.

I have seen many of my dearest friends and associates, men endowed with splendid gifts of intellect and noble qualities of heart, fall, in the prime of life, victims of this dread tyrant; men who, were they yet living, would be ornaments to the world, while their friendship and company would add to my enjoyment in the same proportion as I was caused sorrow by their loss.

Therefore, to prevent so great an evil for the future, I have decided to point out, in this brief treatise, what a fatal abuse is the vice of intemperance, and how easily it may be removed and replaced by the temperate habits of life which were formerly universal. And this I undertake all the more willingly, since I have been pressed thereunto by a number of young men of the brightest intellect, who are well aware that intemperance is a fatal vice; for they have seen their fathers die from its effects in the flower of manhood, while, on the other hand, they behold me still hale and flourishing at my great age of eighty-three years. ,

Now, Nature does not deny us the power of living many years. Indeed, old age, as a matter of fact, is the time of life to be most coveted, as it is then that prudence is best exercised, and the fruits of all the other virtues are enjoyed with the least opposition; because, by that time, the passions are subdued, and man gives himself up wholly to reason.

Hence, being desirous that they likewise may attain old age, these young people have besought me that I may be pleased to tell them the means by which I have been able to reach this advanced age. And since I perceive them full of so honest a desire, and as I heartily wish to benefit not only them, but those others also who may wish to read this brief treatise of mine, I shall now set forth, in writing, the cause which induced me to abandon my intemperate habits, and to embrace the orderly and temperate life. I shall likewise relate the manner in which I went about this reform, and the good results I afterward experienced through it; whence it will be clearly seen how easy a matter it is to overcome the habit of excess. And I shall demonstrate, in conclusion, how much that is good and advantageous is to be derived from the temperate life.

I say, then, that the dire infirmities from which I constantly suffered, and which had not only invaded my system, but had gained such headway as to have become most serious, were the cause of my renouncing the errors of intemperance to which I had been very much addicted.

The excesses of my past life, together with my bad constitution,—my stomach being very cold and moist,—had caused me to fall a prey to various ailments, such as pains in the stomach, frequent pains in the side, symptoms of gout, and, still worse, a low fever that was almost continuous; but I suffered especially from disorder of the stomach, and from an unquenchable thirst. This evil—nay, worse than evil—condition left me nothing to hope for myself, except that death should terminate my troubles and the weariness of my life—a life as yet far removed from its natural end, though brought near to a close by my wrong manner of living.

After every known means of cure had been tried, without affording me any relief, I was, between my thirty-fifth and fortieth years, reduced to so infirm a condition that my physicians declared there was but one remedy left for my ills—a remedy which would surely conquer them, provided I would make up my mind to apply it and persevere patiently in its use.

That remedy was the temperate and orderly life, which, they assured me, possessed as great strength and efficacy for the accomplishment of good results, as that other, which was completely its opposite in every way,—I mean an intemperate and disorderly life,—possessed for doing harm. And of the power of these two opposite manners of living I should entertain no doubt; both by reason of the fact that my infirmities had been caused by disorder,—though, indeed, I was not yet reduced to such extremity that I might not be wholly freed from them by the temperate life, which counteracts the effects of an intemperate one,—and because it is obvious that this regular and orderly life preserves in health even persons of feeble constitution and decrepit age, as long as they observe it. It is equally manifest that the opposite life, an irregular and disorderly one, has the power to ruin, while in the strength of early manhood, the constitutions of men endowed with robustness, and to keep them sick for a great length of time. All this is in

[44]

accordance with the natural law which ordains that contrary ways of living must necessarily produce contrary effects. Art itself, imitating in this the processes of nature, will gradually correct natural defects and imperfections—a principle we find clearly exemplified in agriculture and other similar things.

My physicians warned me, in conclusion, that if I neglected to apply this remedy, in a short time it would be too late to derive any benefit from it; for, in a few months, I should certainly die

I, who was very sad at the thought of dying at so early an age and yet was continually tormented by sickness, having heard these good and plausible reasons, grew thoroughly convinced that from order and from disorder must of necessity proceed the contrary effects which I have mentioned; and, fired with hope, I resolved that, in order to escape death and, at the same time, to be delivered from my sufferings, I would embrace the orderly life.

Having been instructed by my physicians as to the method I was to adopt, I understood that I was not to partake of any foods, either solid or liquid, save such as are prescribed for invalids; and, of these, in small quantities only. To tell the truth, diet had been prescribed for me before; but it had been at a time, when, preferring to live as I pleased and being weary of such foods, I did not refrain from gratifying myself by eating freely of all those things which were to my taste. And being consumed, as it were, by fever, I did not hesitate to continue drinking, and in large quantities, the wines which pleased my palate. Of all this, of course, after the fashion of invalids, I never breathed a word to my physicians.

After I had once taken a firm resolution that I would

Lessons from a 16th-century dieting bestseller

One of the most successful diet books, *The Art of Living Long* by a Venetian merchant named Luigi Cornaro (1464-1566), is still in print more than 450 years after it was first published in Padua in 1558.

It was an instant success, went through many editions, and was translated into many languages. Contemporaries such as Elyot, Boorde, Vaughan and Markham, concerned with what they perceived to be the problem of excessive eating and drinking, had read Cornaro's "admirable diet", a diet not far removed from the simple peasant food they all advocated.

A 1903 edition of *The Art of Living Long* was still advising its readers to take good heed of Cornaro's work, and recommending the spirit of his approach, if not his life-and-death method, the strictness of which could, as today's neurobehaviourists recognise, sometimes backfire.

Cornaro's story is one of sin and redemption, and it begins with a no-holds-barred confession about his first 40 years that were spent in dissipated, gluttonous overindulgence. This way of life had deprived him of many of his excellent friends, so he employed the best physicians to help him undo the self-inflicted damage before he, too, went to an early grave. Eventually the conclusion was reached that only one thing would save him – a sober and regular life. It was diet or die for Cornaro, so he worked out a personal regimen and saved his own life.

The first rule of Cornaro's diet is to

regain self-control. Gluttony, he believed, was not merely a personal idea that "what delights the palate, sin but also a killer. He saw it as an almost apocalyptic force: it "kills every year . . . as great a number as the sensualists who would suffer in the long run and provide business for the "apothecary [who] is perpetually employed in countermining the cook and the sword or fire of many bloody wars".

Citing the ancients, Galen, Hippocrates, Plato and Cicero, he insisted, with the zeal of a convert, on living a regular life of moderation. All passions had to be restrained if not denied, and one should cease to be a slave to pleasure and appetites because they were nothing but fatal delusions.

Taste was one such pleasure. The idea that "what delights the palate, cannot be good for the heart" was false, he wrote, and only served most dreadful pestilence, or by the most dreadful pestilence, or by the vintner". Physic, or medicine, was, for the most part, nothing but a substitute for the actual weight loss necessities of exercise and temperance.

People should eat little and frugally (today's calorie restrictors are Cornaro's direct dieting descendants) he advised, and the recommended a diet consisting of 12oz a day in bread, soups, yolks of new-laid eggs, meat, plus about 14oz of wine.

Extracted from 'Calories and Corsets' by Louise Foxcroft, published this week by Profile Books, £14.99

...k, people are returning to their natural hair colour. By Bethan Cole

recently back to ... ristophe Juliette Thomas, ara Mas- natural do it are he says. ot limited olic eye. to high- as John d Julien kers and essionals ir "cara- brunette" ality. d a trend heir hair ckburne, a. "One ing this ney – to

get an extra month out of their colour before colour maintenance is required. However, most of these clients ask for more natural highlights to be pulled through their hair so that the regrowth isn't as noticeable and the change isn't such a shock."

Farel says: "Woman go back to their natural colour for a variety of reasons. Some are tired of being a slave to their tresses or in today's economy can no longer afford the maintenance required."

Robin says: "They do the colour change for themselves, not to please a man. They are searching for authenticity".

Actress Kiera Chaplin, a natural blonde, says: "I enjoy changing my hair colour but I always end up going back to my natural colour afterwards. I think it's nice to change things up once in a while but blonde suits me best."

EJ Gladstone, who helps run grooming pitstop Butterfly in the City of London says: "A lot of people said that my natural colour [brown] worked much better with my skin tone than the blonde highlights I used to have. I looked less washed out, as I have very pale skin."

Emma Kate Miller, a communications executive, says: "My make-up was never right when I had dyed blonde hair, so I returned to my natural brown shade. I feel so much more like myself."

Robin believes that returning to one's natural colour can make hair "shiny and more dense". This was the case for socialite Olivia Palermo, from US reality show *The City*, for example, who recently returned to her natural ash brown after being blonde for a year and says: "I enjoy my natural colour; my hair is at its healthiest."

The process can be lengthy and costly. Some hairdressers, such as John Frieda, recommend you grow out your dye before returning to "virgin" hair, a process

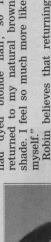

Natural Olivia Palermo   Getty

that can take months and even years. Others, such as the London-based Percy & Reed salon, will use a bleach. Yet others recommend dying hair back to a similar colour to the roots and then allowing it to grow naturally. Whatever technique, expect it to take at least a few hours and cost upwards of £70 with a head colourist in a top salon.

Some people who undergo a return to the roots are not always emotionally prepared for the reaction. Farel says: "Most people who try and go back to their natural colour go into shock because it changes their look completely.

"Also, they usually remember their natural hair colour as different from what it actually is and forget the reason that they started colouring it to begin with: they did not actually like their natural hair colour."

henceforth live temperately and rationally, and had realized, as I did, that to do so was not only an easy matter, but, indeed, the duty of every man, I entered upon my new course so heartily that I never afterward swerved from it, nor ever committed the slightest excess in any direction. Within a few days I began to realize that this new life suited my health excellently; and, persevering in it, in less than a year—though the fact may seem incredible to some—I found myself entirely cured of all my complaints.

Now that I was in perfect health, I began to consider seriously the power and virtue of order; and I said to myself that, as it had been able to overcome so many and such great ills as mine, it would surely be even more efficacious to preserve me in health, to assist my unfortunate constitution, and to strengthen my extremely weak stomach.

Accordingly, I began to observe very diligently what kinds of food agreed with me. I determined, in the first place, to experiment with those which were most agreeable to my palate, in order that I might learn if they were suited to my stomach and constitution. The proverb, "Whatever tastes good will nourish and strengthen," is generally regarded as embodying a truth, and is invoked, as a first principle, by those who are sensually inclined. In it I had hitherto firmly believed; but now I was resolved to test the matter, and find to what extent, if any, it was true.

My experience, however, proved this saying to be false. For instance, dry and very cold wine was agreeable to my taste; as were also melons; and, among other garden produce, raw salads; also fish, pork, tarts, vegetable soups, pastries, and other similar articles. All of these, I say, suited my taste exactly, and yet I found they were hurtful to me. Thus having, by my own experience, proved the proverb in question to be erroneous, I ever after looked upon it as such, and gave up the use of that kind of food and of that kind of wine, as well as cold drinking. Instead, I chose only such wines as agreed with my stomach, taking of them only such a quantity as I knew it could easily digest; and I observed the same rule with regard to my food, exercising care both as to the quantity and the quality. In this manner, I accustomed myself to the habit of never fully satisfying my appetite, either with eating or drinking—always leaving the table well able to take more. In this I acted according to the proverb: *"Not to satiate one's self with food is the science of health."*

Being thus rid, for the reasons and in the manner I have given, of intemperance and disorder, I devoted myself entirely to the sober and regular life. This had such a beneficial effect upon me that, in less than a year as I have just said, I was entirely freed from all the ills which had been so deeply rooted in my system as to have become almost incurable.

Another excellent result which this new life effected in me was that I no longer fell sick every year—as I had always previously done while following my former sensual manner of life—of a strange fever, which at times had brought me near to death's door; but, under my new regimen, from this also was I delivered.

In a word, I grew most healthy; and I have remained so from that time to this day, and for no other reason than that of my constant fidelity to the orderly life. The unbounded virtue of this is, that that which I eat and drink,—always being such as agrees with my constitution and, in quantity, such as it should be,—after it has imparted its invigorating elements to my body, leaves it without any difficulty and without ever generating within it any bad humors Whence, following this rule, as I have already said, I have constantly been, and am now—thank God!—most healthy.

It is true, however, that besides these two very important rules which I have always so carefully observed, relative to eating and drinking,—namely, to take only the quantity which my stomach can easily digest and only the kinds that agree with it,—I have also been careful to guard against great heat and cold, as well as extreme fatigue or excesses of any nature; I have never allowed my accustomed sleep and rest to be interfered with; I have avoided remaining for any length of time in places poorly ventilated; and have been careful not to expose myself too much to the wind or the sun; for these things, too, are great disorders. Yet it is not a very difficult matter to avoid them; for, in a being endowed with reason, the desire of life and health possesses greater weight than the mere pleasure of doing things which are known to be hurtful.

I have also preserved myself, as far as I have been able, from those other disorders from which it is more difficult to be exempt; I mean melancholy, hatred, and the other passions of the soul, which all appear greatly to affect the body. However, my efforts in this direction have not been so successful as to preserve me wholly; since, on more than one occasion. I have been subject to either one or the other of these disturbances, not to say all of them.   Yet even this fact has proved useful to me; for my experience has convinced me that, in reality, these disorders have not much power over, nor can they do much harm to, the bodies of those whose lives are governed by the two rules I have already mentioned relative to eating and drinking. So I can say, with truth, that whosoever observes these two principal rules can suffer but little from any disorder.

Galen,* the famous physician, bore testimony to this truth long before my time. He asserts that all other disorders caused him but very little harm, because he had learned to guard against those of excessive eating and drinking; and that, for this reason, he was never indisposed for more than a day. That this is indeed true I can bear living testimony, corroborated by the statement of everybody who knows me; for my friends, well aware that I have often suffered exposure to cold, heat, and other similar disorders, have also seen me disturbed in mind on account of various misfortunes that have befallen me at different times. Nevertheless, they know that these troubles of mine have harmed me but little; but they can testify to the considerable damage which these very things have brought to others who were not followers of the temperate and regular life.

Among these I may number a brother of mine, and several other near relatives; who, trusting to their good constitutions, did not follow the temperate life—a fact which was the cause of grave harm to them. Their perturbations of mind exercised great influence over their bodies; and such was the anxiety and melancholy with which they were overwhelmed when they saw me involved in certain highly important lawsuits brought against me by men of power and position, and so great was their fear that I should lose, that they were seized with the humor of melancholy, of which the bodies of those who live irregularly are always full. This humor so embittered their lives, and grew upon them to such a degree, that it brought them to the grave before their time.

Yet I suffered nothing throughout it all; for, in me,

* See Note F

[49]

this humor was not excessive. On the contrary, encouraging myself, I tried to believe that God had permitted those lawsuits to be brought against me in order that my own strength and courage might better be made known, and that I should win them to my own advantage and honor; as in fact I eventually did, gaining a glorious and profitable victory. And the very great consolation of soul I then experienced had, in its turn, no power to harm me.

It is thus clear that neither melancholy nor any other disorder can seriously injure bodies governed by the orderly and temperate life. Nay, I shall go still further, and assert that even accidents have the power to do but little harm, or cause but little pain, to the followers of such a life.

The truth of this statement I learned by my own experience at the age of seventy. It happened, one day, while driving at a high rate of speed, I met with an accident. My carriage was overturned, and was dragged quite a distance before the horses could be stopped. Being unable to extricate myself, I was very badly hurt. My head and the rest of my body were painfully bruised, while one of my arms and one of my legs received especially severe injuries.

I was brought home, and my family sent immediately for the doctors; who, when they had come and found me at my advanced age so shaken and in so bad a plight, could not help giving their opinion that I would die within three days.

They suggested two things, however, as their only hopes for my recovery: one was bleeding, the other was purging; in order, as they said, to cleanse my system and thus prevent the alteration of the humors, which they expected at any moment to become so much dis-

JOSEPH ADDISON
1672—1719

From the painting by Sir Godfrey Kneller—No. 283, National Portrait Gallery,
London

Photograph copyrighted by Walker and Cockerell

turbed as to produce high fever. I, nevertheless, convinced that the regular life I had led for many years had united, equalized, and disposed all my humors so well that they could not possibly be subject to so great alteration, refused either to be bled or to take any medicine. I merely had my arm and leg straightened, and permitted my body to be rubbed with certain oils which were recommended by the physicians as appropriate under the circumstances. It followed that, without using any other kind of remedy and without suffering any further ill or change for the worse, I entirely recovered—a thing, which, while fulfilling my own expectations, seemed to my doctors nothing less than miraculous.

The unavoidable conclusion to be drawn from this is, that any man who leads the regular and temperate life, not swerving from it in the least degree where his nourishment is concerned, can be but little affected by other disorders or incidental mishaps. Whereas, on the other hand, I truly conclude that disorderly habits of living are those which are fatal.

By a recent experience of mine—that is, as late as four years ago—this was proved to me unmistakably. Having been induced by the advice of my physicians, the admonitions of my friends and their loving exhortations, to make a change in my manner of living, I found this change—consisting in an increase in the ordinary quantity of my food—to be, in reality, a disorder of much greater importance than might have been expected; since it brought on me a most severe illness. As the whole event is appropriate here, and because the knowledge of it may be of advantage to others, I shall now relate it in all its particulars.

My dearest relatives and friends, who love and cherish me devotedly and are inspired by warm and true

[53]

affection, observed how very little I ate, and, in unison with my physicians, told me that the food I took could not possibly be sufficient to sustain a man of an age so advanced as mine. They argued that I should not only preserve, but rather aim to increase, my strength and vigor. And as this could only be done by means of nourishment, it was absolutely necessary, they said, that I should eat rather more abundantly.

I, on the other hand, brought forward my reasons to the contrary; namely, that nature is satisfied with little; that my spare diet had been found sufficient to preserve me in health all these many years; and that, with me, this abstemious habit had long since become second nature. I maintained, furthermore, that it was in harmony with reason that, as my age increased and my strength lessened, I should diminish, rather than increase, the quantity of my food. This was true; since the digestive powers of the stomach were also growing weaker in the same proportion as my vigor became impaired. Wherefore I could see no reason why I should increase my diet.

To strengthen my argument, I quoted those two natural and obviously true proverbs: the one, that *"Whosoever wishes to eat much must eat little"*—which means simply that the eating of little lengthens a man's life, and by living a long time he is enabled to eat a great deal; the other, that *"The food from which a man abstains, after he has eaten heartily, is of more benefit to him than that which he has eaten."*

However, neither of these wise sayings, nor any other argument I could offer, proved effectual; for my friends only pressed me the harder. Now, I did not like to appear obstinate or as though I considered myself more of a doctor than the very doctors themselves;

moreover, I especially wished to please my family, who
desired it very earnestly, believing, as they did, that
such an increase in my ordinary allowance would be
beneficial to my strength. So I at last yielded, and con-
sented to add to the quantity of my food. This increase,
however, was by only two ounces in weight; so that,
while, with bread, the yolk of an egg, a little meat, and
some soup, I had formerly eaten as much as would weigh
in all exactly twelve ounces, I now went so far as to
raise the amount to fourteen ounces; and, while I had
formerly drunk but fourteen ounces of wine, I now began
to take sixteen ounces.

The disorder of this increase had, at the end of ten
days, begun to affect me so much, that, instead of being
cheerful, as I had ever been, I became melancholy and
choleric; everything annoyed me, and my mood was so
wayward that I neither knew what to say to others nor
what to do with myself. At the end of twelve days I
was seized with a most violent pain in the side, which
continued twenty-two hours. This was followed by a
terrible fever, which lasted thirty-five days and as many
nights without a moment's interruption; although, to
tell the truth, it kept constantly diminishing after the
fifteenth day. Notwithstanding such abatement, however, during all that period I was never able to sleep for
even half of a quarter of an hour; hence, everybody
believed that I would surely die. However, I recovered
—God be praised!—solely by returning to my former
rule of life; although I was then seventy-eight years of
age, and it was just in the heart of the coldest season of
a very cold year, and I as frail in body as could be.

I am firmly convinced that nothing rescued me from
death but the orderly life which I had observed for so
many years; in all of which time no kind of sickness had

ever visited me, unless I may call by that name some
slight indisposition lasting a day or two only. The
steady rule of life I had so long observed had not,
as I have already said, allowed the generation of any
evil or excessive humors in my body; or, if any had been
formed, it had not permitted them to acquire strength
or to become malignant, as is the case in the bodies of
old persons who live without restraint. Consequently,
as in my system there was none of that chronic viciousness of humors which kills men, but only that new condition brought about by my recent irregularity, this
attack of illness—although indeed very serious—was not
able to cause my death.

This, and nothing else, was the means of my recovery; whence we may judge how great are the power and
virtue of order, and how great is the power of disorder—
the latter having been able, in a few days, to bring upon
me a sickness which proved to be so terrible; whereas
the regular and temperate life had maintained me in perfect health during so many years. And it seems to me
most reasonable that, if the world is maintained by
order, and if our life is nothing else—so far as the body
is concerned—but the harmony and order of the four
elements, it must follow that only through this same
order can our life be sustained; while, on the other
hand, it is ruined by sickness or dissolved by death,
according as this order is not observed. It is through
order that the sciences are more easily mastered; it is
order that gives the victory to armies; and, finally, it is
due to order that the stability of families, of cities, and
even of governments, is maintained.

Therefore I conclude that orderly living is the most
positive law and foundation of a long and healthy life.
We may say it is the true and only medicine; and who-

ever considers all this deliberately must declare it is
indeed so.

When a physician pays a visit to a sick man, he pre-
scribes this as the very first condition of recovery, urging
him, above all things, to live the orderly life. In like
manner, when he bids good-bye to his patient upon his
recovery, he recommends, as a means of preserving
restored health, that he continue this orderly life. And
there is no doubt that if the one so advised were to act
accordingly, he would avoid all sickness in the future;
because a well-regulated life removes the causes of
disease. Thus, for the remainder of his days, he would
have no further need either of doctors or of medicines.

Moreover, by applying his mind to this matter which
should so deeply concern him, he would become his own
physician, and, indeed, the only perfect one he could
have; for it is true that *"A man cannot be a perfect
physician of any one save of himself alone."*

The reason of this is that any man may, by dint of
experimenting, acquire a perfect knowledge of his own
constitution and of its most hidden qualities, and find
out what food and what drink, and what quantities of
each, will agree with his stomach. It is impossible to have
equally accurate knowledge of these things in another
person; since it is only with difficulty that we may discover them in ourselves. And to learn them in our own
cases, great attention, considerable time, and much study
are required. Nor must we overlook the fact that
various experiments are absolutely necessary; for there
is not so great a variety of features as there is diversity
of temperaments and stomachs among men.

Who would believe, for instance, that wine over a
year old would be hurtful to my stomach, while new wine
would be suitable to it? and that pepper, which is com-

monly considered a heating spice, would not act upon me as such, but that cinnamon would warm and help me? What physician could have informed me of these two hidden qualities of my nature; since I myself, after a long course of observation, have barely been able to note and find them?

Therefore, I say again, from all these reasons it follows that it is impossible for anyone to be a perfect physician of another. Since, then, a man can have no better doctor than himself, and no better medicine than the temperate life, he should by all means embrace that life.

I do not mean to say, however, that in the knowledge and treatment of the diseases incurred by those who do not lead orderly lives, there is no need of the physician, or that he should not be valued highly. For, if a friend brings comfort when he comes to us in time of sickness, —though his visit be merely to manifest sympathy in our suffering and to encourage us to hope for recovery,— how much the more ought we to appreciate the physician who is a friend visiting us that he may be of service, and who promises to restore our health? Yet, when it comes to a question of preserving health, my opinion is that we should take, as our proper physician, the regular and temperate life. For, as we have seen, it is the true medicine of nature and best suited to man; it keeps him in health, even though he be of an unfortunate constitution; it enables him to retain his strength to the age of a hundred years or more; and, finally, it does not suffer him to pass away through sickness or by any alteration of the humors, but simply by the coming to an end of the radical moisture, which is exhausted at the last. Learned men have often asserted that similar effects could be obtained by means of drinkable gold or the "elixir of life"; yet, though they have thus been sought by many, who have found them?

Let us be truthful. Men are, as a rule, very sensual and intemperate, and wish to gratify their appetites and give themselves up to the commission of innumerable disorders. When, seeing that they cannot escape suffering the unavoidable consequence of such intemperance as often as they are guilty of it, they say—by way of excuse—that it is preferable to live ten years less and to enjoy one's life. They do not pause to consider what immense importance ten years more of life, and especially of healthy life, possess when we have reached mature age, the time, indeed, at which men appear to the best advantage in learning and virtue—two things which can never reach their perfection except with time. To mention nothing else at present, I shall only say that, in literature and in the sciences, the majority of the best and most celebrated works we possess were written when their authors had attained ripe age, and during those same ten latter years for which some men, in order that they may gratify their appetites, say they do not care.

Be this as it may, I have not chosen to imitate them; on the contrary, I have chosen to live these ten years Had I not done so, I should never have written the treatises, which, as I have been alive and well, I have been able to write during the last ten years; and that they will prove useful I have no doubt.

Furthermore, the aforesaid followers of sensuality will tell you that the temperate and orderly life is an impossible one. To which I answer: Galen, great as a physician, led it, and chose it as the best medicine. So, likewise, did Plato, Cicero, Isocrates, and many other famous men in times past; whose names, lest I grow

[59]

tedious, I shall forbear to mention. In our own time, we have seen Pope Paul Farnese [1468-1549] and Cardinal Bembo [1470-1547] lead this life, and for this reason attain great age; the same may be said of our two Doges,* Lando [1462-1545] and Donato [1468-1553]. Besides these, we might mention many others in humbler states and conditions, not only in the cities, but in the country also; for in every place there are to be found those who follow the temperate life, and always to their own considerable advantage.

Seeing, therefore, that it has been practiced in the past, and that many are now practicing it, the temperate life is clearly proved to be one easily followed; and all the more so by reason of the fact that it does not call for any great exertion. Indeed—as is stated by the abovementioned Cicero and by all who follow it—the only difficulty, if any there be, consists in making a beginning.

Plato, himself living the temperate life, nevertheless declares that a man in the service of the State cannot lead it; because he is often compelled to suffer heat and cold and fatigues of various kinds, as well as other hardships, all contrary to the temperate life, and in themselves disorders. Yet, I repeat the assertion I have already made, that these disorders are not of any great consequence, and are powerless to cause grievous sickness or death, provided he who is obliged to suffer them leads an abstemious life, and is never guilty of any excess in eating or drinking. Excess is a thing which any man, even one who is in the service of the State, can very well avoid, and must, indeed, necessarily avoid; since by so doing he may rest assured, either that he will never incur those ills into which it would otherwise be easy for him to fall while committing disorders which are brought upon him in the discharge of his duties, or

* See Note G

[60]

that he will be able the more easily and quickly to free himself of those ills, should he, perchance, be overtaken by them.

Here one might object—as some actually do—that a man accustomed to lead the temperate life, having always, while in sound health, partaken of food proper for sick persons, and in small quantities only, has nothing left to fall back upon in time of sickness.

To this objection I shall answer, in the first place, that Nature, being desirous to preserve man as long as possible, teaches him what rule to follow in time of illness; for she immediately deprives the sick of their appetite in order that they may eat but little—for with little, as it has already been said, Nature is content. Consequently, whether the sick man, up to the time of his illness, has led the orderly or a disorderly life, it is necessary that he should then partake of such food only as is suited to his condition, and, in quantity, less of it than he was wont to take when in health. Should he, when ill, continue to eat the same amount as when in health, he would surely die; while, were he to eat more, he would die all the sooner. For his natural powers, already oppressed with sickness, would thereby be burdened beyond endurance, having had forced upon them a quantity of food greater than they could support under the circumstances. A reduced quantity is, in my opinion, all that is required to sustain the invalid.

Another answer to this objection—and a better one—is, that he who leads the temperate life can never fall sick, or at least can do so only rarely; and his indisposition lasts but a very short while. For, by living temperately, he removes all the causes of illness; and, having removed these, he thereby removes the effects. So the man who lives the orderly life should have no fear of sickness; for surely he has no reason to fear an effect, the cause of which is under his own control.

Now, since the orderly life is, as we have seen, so useful, so potent, so beautiful, and so holy, it should be embraced and followed by every rational being, and this all the more from the fact that it is a life very easy to lead, and one that does not conflict with the career of any condition of man.

No one need feel obliged to confine himself to the small quantity to which I limit myself; nor to abstain from fruit, fish, and other things which I do not take. For I eat but little; and my reason in doing so is that I find a little sufficient for my small and weak stomach. Moreover, as fruit, fish, and similar foods disagree with me, I do not use them. Persons, however, with whom these do agree may—nay, should—partake of them; for to such they are by no means forbidden. That which is forbidden to them and to everybody else, is to partake of food, even though it be of the kind suited to them, in a quantity so large that it cannot be easily digested, and the same is true with regard to drink. But should there be a man to whom no kind of food is harmful, he, obviously, would not be subject to the rule of quality, but must needs regard only that of quantity—an observance which becomes a very easy matter.

I do not wish to be told here that among those who lead the most irregular lives there are men, who, in spite of this fact, reach, healthy and robust, those furthest limits of life attained by the temperate; for this argument is grounded upon a position uncertain and dangerous, and upon a fact, moreover, which is of so rare occurrence that, when it does occur, it appears more a miracle than a natural result. Hence it should not persuade us to live disorderly lives; for Nature was merely unwontedly liberal to those irregular livers, and very few of us can, or should, hope that she will be as bountiful to us.

He who, trusting to his youth or his strong constitution and perfect stomach, will not take proper care of himself, loses a great deal, and every day is exposed, in consequence of his intemperate life, to sickness and even death. For this reason I maintain that an old man who lives regularly and temperately, even though he be of poor constitution, is more likely to live than is a young man of perfect health if addicted to disorderly habits.

There is no doubt, of course, that a man blessed with a strong constitution will be able to preserve himself longer by living the temperate life than he who has a poor one; and it is also true that God and Nature can cause men to be brought into the world with so perfect constitutions that they will live for many years in health, without observing this strict rule of life. A case of this kind is that of the Procurator* Thomas Contarini of Venice [1454-1554], and another is that of the Knight Anthony Capodivacca of Padua [1465?-1555]. But such instances are so rare that, it is safe to say, there is not more than one man in a hundred thousand of whom it will prove true.

The universal rule is that they who wish not only constantly to enjoy perfect health and to attain their full limit of life, but finally to pass away without pain or difficulty and of mere exhaustion of the radical moisture, must lead the temperate life; for upon this condition, and no other, will they enjoy the fruits of such a life—fruits almost innumerable, and each one to be infinitely prized. For as sobriety keeps the humors of the body pure and mild, so, likewise, does it prevent

* See Note H

fumes from arising from the stomach to the head; and the brain of him who lives in this manner is, as a result, constantly in a clear condition, permitting him to maintain entire the use of reason. Thus, to his own extreme comfort and contentment, is he enabled to rise above the low and mean considerations of this world to the high and beautiful contemplation of things divine. In this manner he considers, knows, and understands, as he never would have otherwise done, how great are the power, the wisdom, and the goodness of God. Descending thence to the realms of Nature, he recognizes in her the daughter of the same God; and he sees and touches that which at any other age of his life, or with a less purified mind, he could never have seen or touched.

Then, indeed, does he fully realize the ugliness of vice, into which those persons fall who have not learned to control their passions or to bridle those three importunate desires which seem, all three together, to be born with us in order to keep us forever troubled and disturbed—the desires of carnal pleasures, of honors, and of worldly possessions. These lusts appear to increase with age in those who are not followers of the temperate life; because, when passing through the years of earlier manhood, they did not relinquish, as they should have done, either sensuality or appetite, to embrace in their stead reason and self-control—virtues which followers of the temperate life never abandoned in their years of strength.

On the contrary, these more fortunate men, well knowing that such passions and desires are irrational, and having given themselves wholly to reason, were freed both of their tyranny and at the same time of all other vices, and drawn, instead, to virtue and good works. By this means, from the vicious men they had once been, they became true and upright. At length, in process of time and owing to extreme age, their dissolution and close of life are near at hand. Yet, conscious that they have, through God's special grace, abandoned the ways of vice and ever afterward followed those of virtue, and firmly hoping, moreover, through the merits of Jesus Christ our Redeemer, to die in His grace, they are not saddened by the thought of the approach of death, which they know to be unavoidable.

This is especially the case when, loaded with honors and satiated with life, they perceive they have reached that age which scarcely any man—among the many thousands born into this world—who follows a different mode of living, ever attains. And the inevitable approach of death grieves them so much the less in that it does not come suddenly or unexpectedly, with a troublesome and bitter alteration of the humors, and with sharp pains and cruel fever; but it comes most quietly and mildly. For, in them, the end is caused merely by the failure of the radical moisture; which, consumed by degrees, finally becomes completely exhausted, after the manner of a lamp which gradually fails. Hence they pass away peacefully, and without any kind of sickness, from this earthly and mortal life to the heavenly and eternal one.

O holy and truly happy Temperate Life, most worthy to be looked upon as such by all men! even as the other, disorderly and so contrary to thee, is sinful and wretched—as those who will but stop to reflect upon the opposite effects of both must clearly see. Thy lovely name alone should be sufficient to bring men to a knowledge of thee; for thy name, The Orderly and Temperate Life, is beautiful to speak; while how offensive are the words *disorder* and *intemperance!*

Indeed, between the very mention of these two opposites lies the same difference as between those other two, *angel* and *devil*.

I have so far given the reasons for which I abandoned disorder and devoted myself wholly to the temperate life; also the manner in which I went about it that I might accomplish my end; together with the subsequent effects of this change; and, finally, I have attempted to describe the advantages and blessings which the temperate life bestows on those who follow it.

And now, since some sensual and unreasonable men pretend that long life is not a blessing or a thing to be desired, but that the existence of a man after he has passed the age of sixty-five cannot any longer be called a living life, but rather should be termed a dead one, I shall plainly show they are much mistaken; for I have an ardent desire that every man should strive to attain my age, in order that he may enjoy what I have found—and what others, too, will find—to be the most beautiful period of life.

For this purpose I wish to speak here of the pastimes and pleasures which I enjoy at this advanced season of life. I desire, in this manner, openly to bear witness to all mankind—and every person who knows me will testify to the truth of what I say—that the life which I am now living is a most vital one, and by no means a dead one; and that it is deemed, by many, a life as full of happiness as this world can give.

Those who know me well will give this testimony, in the first place, because they see, and not without the greatest admiration and amazement, how strong I am; that I am able to mount my horse without assistance; and with what ease and agility I can not only ascend a flight of stairs, but also climb a whole hill on foot.

They also see how I am ever cheerful, happy, and contented—free from all perturbations of the soul and from every vexatious thought, instead of these, joy and peace have fixed their abode in my heart, and never depart from it. Moreover, my friends know how I spend my time, and that it is always in such a manner that life does not grow tedious to me; they see that there is no single hour of it that I am not able to pass with the greatest possible delight and pleasure.

Frequently I have the opportunity to converse with many honorable gentlemen; among them, a number who are renowned for their intellect and refinement, and distinguished by their literary attainments, or are of excellence in some other way. When their conversation fails me, I enjoy the time in reading some good book. Having read as much as I care to, I write; endeavoring in this, as in what other manner soever I may, to be of assistance to others, as far as is in my power.

All these things I do with the greatest ease and at my leisure, at their proper seasons, in my own residence; which, besides being situated in the most beautiful quarter of this noble and learned city of Padua, is, in itself, really handsome and worthy of praise—truly a home, the like of which is no longer built in our day. It is so arranged that in one part of it I am protected against the great heat of summer, and in the other part against the extreme cold of winter; for I built the house according to the principles of architecture, which teach us how that should be done. In addition to the mansion, I enjoy my various gardens, beautified by running streams —retreats wherein I always find some pleasant occupation for my time.

I have, besides this, another mode of recreating myself. Every year, in April and May, as well as in

September and October, I spend a few days at a country-seat of mine, situated in the most desirable part of the Euganean Hills.* It is adorned with beautiful gardens and fountains; and I especially delight in its extremely comfortable and fine dwelling. In this spot I also take part, at times, in some easy and pleasant hunting, such as is suited to my age.

For as many days again, I enjoy my villa in the plain. It is very beautiful, both on account of its fine streets converging into a large and handsome square,—in the center of which stands the church, a structure well befitting the place and much honored,—as also because it is divided by a large and rapid branch of the river Brenta, on either side of which spread large tracts of land, all laid out in fertile and carefully cultivated fields. This district is now—God be praised!—exceedingly well populated; for it is, indeed, a very different place from what it was formerly, having once been marshy and of unwholesome atmosphere—a home fit rather for snakes than for human beings. But, after I had drained off the waters, the air became healthful and people flocked thither from every direction; the number of the inhabitants began to multiply exceedingly; and the country was brought to the perfect condition in which it is to-day. Hence I can say, with truth, that in this place I have given to God an altar, a temple, and souls to adore Him. All these are things which afford me infinite pleasure, solace, and contentment every time I return thither to see and enjoy them.

At those same times every year, I go, as well, to revisit some of the neighboring cities, in order that I may enjoy the society of those of my friends whom I find there; for I derive great pleasure from conversing with them. I meet, in their company, men distinguished

* See Note I

for their intellect—architects, painters, sculptors, musicians, and agriculturists; for our times have certainly produced a considerable number of these. I behold, for the first time, their more recent works, and see again their former ones; and I always learn things which it is agreeable and pleasing to me to know. I see the palaces, the gardens, the antiquities, and, together with these, the squares, the churches, and the fortresses; for I endeavor to omit nothing from which I can derive either delight or information.

My greatest enjoyment, in the course of my journeys going and returning, is the contemplation of the beauty of the country and of the places through which I travel. Some of these are in the plains; others on the hills, near rivers or fountains; and all are made still more beautiful by the presence of many charming dwellings surrounded by delightful gardens.

Nor are these my diversions and pleasures rendered less sweet and less precious through the failing of my sight or my hearing, or because any one of my senses is not perfect; for they are all—thank God!—most perfect. This is true especially of my sense of taste; for I now find more true relish in the simple food I eat, wheresoever I may chance to be, than I formerly found in the most delicate dishes at the time of my intemperate life. Neither does the change of bed affect me in the slightest degree; for I always sleep soundly and quietly in what place soever I may happen to be—nothing disturbs me, so that my dreams are always happy and pleasant.

With the greatest delight and satisfaction, also, do I behold the success of an undertaking highly important to our State; namely, the fitting for cultivation of its waste tracts of country, numerous as they were. This improvement was commenced at my suggestion; yet I

[69]

had scarcely ventured to hope that I should live to see it, knowing, as I do, that republics are slow to begin enterprises of great importance. Nevertheless, I have lived to see it. And I was myself present with the members of the committee appointed to superintend the work, for two whole months, at the season of the greatest heat of summer, in those swampy places; nor was I ever disturbed either by fatigue or by any hardship I was obliged to incur. So great is the power of the orderly life which accompanies me wheresoever I may go!

Furthermore, I cherish a firm hope that I shall live to witness not only the beginning, but also the completion, of another enterprise, the success of which is no less important to our beloved Venice; namely, the protection of our estuary, or lagoon, that strongest and most wonderful bulwark of my dear country. The preservation of this—and be it said not through self-complacency, but wholly and purely for truth's sake—has been advised by me repeatedly, both by word of mouth and by carefully written reports to our Republic; for as I owe to her, by right, the fullest means of assistance and benefit that I can give, so also do I most fondly desire to see her enjoy prolonged and enduring happiness, and to know that her security is assured.

These are the true and important recreations, these the comforts and pastimes, of my old age, which is much more to be prized than the old age or even the youth of other men; since it is free, by the grace of God, from all the perturbations of the soul and the infirmities of the body, and is not subject to any of those troubles which woefully torment so many young men and so many languid and utterly worn-out old men.

If to great and momentous things it be proper to

[70]

compare lesser ones, or rather those, I should say, which
are by many considered as hardly worthy of notice, I
shall mention, as another fruit which I have gathered
from the temperate life, that at my present age of eighty-
three I have been able to compose a delightful comedy,
full of innocent mirth and pleasant sayings—a manner of
poem, which, as we all know, is usually the fruit and
production of youth only, just as tragedy is the work of
old age; the former, because of its grace and joyousness,
is more in harmony with the early years of life, while the
melancholy character of the latter is better suited to old
age. Now, if that good old man, a Greek and a poet
[Sophocles], was so highly commended for having written
a tragedy at the age of seventy-three, and was, by reason
of this deed, regarded as vigorous and sound minded,—
although tragedy, as I have just said, is a sad and
melancholy form of poetry,—why should I be deemed
less fortunate or less hale than he, when I have, at an age
greater than his by ten years, written a comedy, which, as
everybody knows, is a cheerful and witty kind of composition? Assuredly, if I am not an unfair judge of myself, I must believe that I am now more vigorous and
more cheerful than was that poet when burdened with ten
years less of life.

In order that nothing be wanting to the fullness of
my consolation, to render my great age less irksome, or to
increase my happiness, I am given the additional comfort
of a species of immortality in the succession of my
descendants. For, as often as I return home, I find
awaiting me not one or two, but eleven, grandchildren, all
the offspring of one father and mother, and all blessed
with perfect health; the eldest is eighteen years of age,
the youngest, two; and, as far as can now be judged, all
are fond of study and inclined to good habits. Among

[71]

the younger ones, I always enjoy some one as my little
jester; for, truly, between the ages of three and five, the
little folks are natural merrymakers. The older children
I look upon as, in a certain way, my companions; and, as
Nature has blessed them with perfect voices, I am
delighted with their singing, and with their playing on
various instruments. Indeed, I often join in their
singing; for my voice is now better, clearer, and more
sonorous than it ever was before.

Such, then, are the pastimes of my old age; and from
these it may readily be seen that the life I am leading is
alive and not dead, as those persons say who are ignorant
of what they are speaking. To whom, in order that I may
make it clearly understood how I regard other people's
manner of living, I truly declare that I would not be
willing to exchange either my life or my great age with
that of any young man, though he be of excellent
constitution, who leads a sensual life; for I well know that
such a one is, as I have already stated, exposed every
day—nay, every hour—to a thousand kinds of infirmity
and death.

This is a fact so obviously clear that it has no need of
proof; for I remember right well what I used to do when
I was like them. I know how very thoughtless that age
is wont to be, and how young men, incited by their inward
fire, are inclined to be daring and confident of themselves
in their actions, and how hopeful they are in every
circumstance; as much on account of the little experience
they have of things past, as because of the certainty they
feel of living long in the future. Thus it is that they
boldly expose themselves to every kind of peril. Putting
aside reason, and giving up the ruling of themselves to
sensuality, they seek with eagerness for means by which
to gratify every one of their appetites, without perceiving
—unfortunate wretches!—that they are bringing upon

themselves the very things which are most unwelcome: not only sickness, as I have said many times, but also death.

Of these evils, sickness is grievous and troublesome to suffer; and the other, which is death, is altogether unbearable and frightful—certainly to any man who has given himself up a prey to sensuality, and especially to young people, to whom it seems that they lose too much in dying before their time. And it is indeed frightful to those who reflect upon the errors with which this mortal life of ours is filled, and upon the vengeance which the justice of God is liable to take in the eternal punishment of the wicked.

I, on the contrary, old as I am, find myself—thanks always to Almighty God!—entirely free of both the one and the other of these two cares: of the one, sickness, because I know to a certainty I cannot ever fall sick, the holy medicine of the temperate life having removed from me forever all the causes of illness; and of the other, namely, of death, because I have learned, through a practice of many years, to give full play to reason. Wherefore I not only deem it wrong to fear that which cannot be avoided, but I also firmly hope that, when the hour of my passing away is come, I shall feel the consoling power of the grace of Jesus Christ.

Moreover, although I am fully aware that I, like everybody else, must come to that end which is inevitable, yet it is still so far away that I cannot discern it. For I am certain there is no death in store for me save that of mere dissolution; since the regular method of my life has closed all other avenues to the approach of death, and has prevented the humors of my body from waging against me any other war than that arising from the elements of which my body was originally formed.

[73]

I am not so unwise as not to know that, having been born, I must die. Yet beautiful and desirable, indeed, is that death which Nature provides for us by way of the dissolution of the elements; both because she herself, having formed the bond of life, finds more easily the way to loose it, and also because she delays the end longer than would the violence of disease. Such is the death, which, without playing the poet, alone deserves the name of death, as arising from Nature's laws. It cannot be otherwise; for it comes only after a very long span of life, and then solely as the result of extreme weakness. Little by little, very slowly, men are reduced to such a state that they find themselves no longer able to walk, and scarcely to reason; moreover, they become blind, deaf, and bent, and afflicted with every other kind of infirmity. But, so far as I am concerned, I feel certain that not only will my end, by the blessing of God, be very different, but also that my soul, which has so agreeable a habitation in my body, —where it finds nothing but peace, love, and harmony, not only between the humors, but also between the senses and reason,—rejoices and abides in it in a state of such complete contentment, that it is only reasonable to believe it will require much time and the weight of many years to force it to leave. Wherefore I may fairly conclude there is yet in store for me a long continuance of perfect health and strength, wherein I may enjoy this beautiful world, which is indeed beautiful to those who know how to make it so for themselves, as I have done And I treasure the hope that, through the grace of God, I shall also be able to enjoy the other world beyond. All this is solely by means of virtue, and of the holy life of order which I adopted when I became the friend of reason and the enemy of sensuality and appetite—an adoption which may easily be made by any man who wishes to live as becomes a man.

Now, if the temperate life is such a happy one, if its name is so beautiful and lovable, if the possession of it is so certain and so secure, there is nothing left for me to do except to entreat—since by oratorical persuasion I cannot attain my desire—every man endowed with gentle soul and gifted with rational faculties, to embrace this the richest treasure of life; for as it surpasses all the other riches and treasures of this world by giving us a long and healthy life, so it deserves to be loved, sought after, and preserved always by all.

Divine Sobriety, pleasing to God, the friend of nature, the daughter of reason, the sister of virtue, the companion of temperate living; modest, agreeable, contented with little, orderly and refined in all her operations! From her, as from a root, spring life, health, cheerfulness, industry, studiousness, and all those actions which are worthy of a true and noble soul. All laws, both divine and human, favor her. From her presence flee— as so many clouds from the sunshine—reveling, disorders, gluttony, excessive humors, indispositions, fevers, pains, and the dangers of death. Her beauty attracts every noble mind. Her security promises to all her followers a graceful and enduring life. Her happiness invites each one, with but little trouble, to the acquisition of her victories. And, finally, she pledges herself to be a kind and benevolent guardian of the life of every human being—of the rich as well as of the poor; of man as of woman; of the old as of the young. To the rich she teaches modesty, to the poor thrift; to man continence, to woman chastity; to the old how to guard against death, and to the young how to hope more firmly and more securely for length of days. Sobriety purifies the senses: lightens the body; quickens the intellect; cheers the mind; makes the memory tenacious, the motions swift, the

[75]

actions ready and prompt. Through her, the soul, almost
delivered of its earthly burden, enjoys to a great extent
its liberty; the vital spirits move softly in the arteries;
the blood courses through the veins; the heat of the body,
always mild and temperate, produces mild and temperate
effects; and, finally, all our faculties preserve, with most
beautiful order, a joyous and pleasing harmony.

O most holy and most innocent Sobriety, the sole
refreshment of nature, the loving mother of human life,
the true medicine both of the soul and of the body; how
much should men praise and thank thee for thy courteous
gifts! Thou givest them the means of preserving life in
health, that blessing than which it did not please God we
should have a greater in this world—life and existence, so
naturally prized, so willingly guarded by every living
creature!

As it is not my intention to make, at this time, a
panegyric on this rare and excellent virtue, and in order
that I may be moderate, even in its regard, I shall bring
this treatise to a close; not that infinitely more might not
yet be said in its behalf than I have said already, but
because it is my wish to postpone the remainder of its
praises to another occasion.

THE SECOND DISCOURSE

Wherein the author further dwells upon the vital neces-

sity of temperate and regular habits of life as

the only means of securing or

preserving perfect health

MY treatise, "The Temperate Life," has begun, as I
desired it should, to render great service to many
of those persons born with weak constitutions,
who, for this reason, feel so very sick whenever they
commit the slightest excess, that they could not possibly
feel worse—a thing, which, it must be allowed, does not
happen to those who are born with robust constitutions.
A number of these delicate persons, having read the
above-mentioned treatise, have commenced to follow the
regular mode of life therein recommended by me, convinced by experience of its beneficial influence.

And now, in like manner, I desire to benefit those
fortunately born with strong constitutions, who, relying
too much upon that fact, lead irregular lives; in conse-

quence of which, by the time they reach the age of sixty or thereabout, they become afflicted with various distressing ills. Some suffer with the gout, some with pains in the side, and others with pains in the stomach or with other complaints; yet with none of these would they ever be troubled were they to lead the temperate life. And, as they now die of these infirmities before reaching their eightieth year, they would, in the contrary case, live to the age of one hundred, the term of life granted by God, and by our mother Nature, to us her children; for it is but reasonable to believe the wish of this excellent mother is that every one of us should attain that natural limit, in order to enjoy the blessings of every period of life.

Our birth is subject to the revolutions of the heavens, which have great power over it, especially with regard to the formation of good and bad constitutions. This is a condition which Nature cannot alter; for, if she could, she would provide that all be born with robust constitutions. She hopes, however, that man, being gifted with intellect and reason, will himself supply by art that which the heavens have denied him; and that, by means of the temperate life, he may succeed in freeing himself of his bad constitution, and be enabled to enjoy a long life in the possession of unvarying perfect health. And there is no doubt that man can, by means of art, free himself partially from the control of the heavens, the common opinion being that, while they influence, they do not compel us. Hence have we that saying of the learned: *"The wise man has power over the stars."*

I was born with a very choleric disposition, insomuch that it was impossible for any person to deal with me. But I recognized the fact, and reflected that a wrathful man is no less than insane at times, that is to say, when

[78]

he is under the sway of his furious passions, he is devoid of both intellect and reason. I resolved, through the exercise of reason, to rid myself of my passionate temper; and I succeeded so well that now—though, as I have said, I am naturally inclined to anger—I never allow myself to give way to it, or, at most, only in a slight degree.

Any man, who, by nature, is of a bad constitution, may similarly, through the use of reason and the help of the temperate life, enjoy perfect health to a very great age; just as I have done, although my constitution was naturally so wretched that it seemed impossible I should live beyond the age of forty. Whereas, I am now in my eighty-sixth year, full of health and strength; and, were it not for the long and severe illnesses with which I was visited so frequently during my youth and which were so serious that the physicians at times despaired of saving me, I should have hoped to reach the above-mentioned term of a hundred years. But, through those illnesses, I lost a large part of my radical moisture; and, as this loss can never be repaired, reason teaches that it will be impossible for me to reach the extreme term. Therefore, as I shall show later on, I never give the matter a thought. It is quite enough for me that I have lived forty-six years longer than I could reasonably have expected; and that, at such an advanced age as mine, all my senses and organs remain in perfect condition—even my teeth, my voice, my memory, and my heart. And as for my brain, it, especially, is more active now than it ever was. Nor do these powers suffer any decline with the increase of years —a blessing to be attributed solely to the fact of my increasing the temperateness of my life.

For, as my years multiply, I lessen the quantity of my food; since, indeed, this decrease is absolutely necessary and cannot be avoided. We cannot live forever; and, as the end of life draws near, man is reduced by degrees to that state in which he is no longer able to eat anything at all, save it may be to swallow, and that with difficulty, the yolk of an egg each day. Thus, as I am confident I shall do, he closes his career by mere dissolution of the elements and without any pain or illness. This, certainly a most desirable lot, is one that will be granted to all, of what degree or condition soever, who lead the temperate life, whether they occupy a high position, or that of the middle class, or are found in the humblest ranks of life; for we all belong to one species, and are composed of the same four elements.

And, since a long and healthy life is a blessing to be highly valued by man, as I shall hereafter explain, I conclude he is in duty bound to do all in his power to attain it   Nor should any hope to enjoy this blessing of longevity without the means of the temperate life, even though they may have heard it said that some who did not live temperately, but, on the contrary, ate much of every kind of food and drank large quantities of wine, have lived, in the enjoyment of health, to see their hundredth year. For, in holding out to themselves the hope that this good fortune will, in like manner, be vouchsafed to them also, they make two mistakes: in the first place, there is scarcely one man in a hundred thousand, who, living such a life, ever attains that happiness; and, secondly, the intemperate sicken and die in consequence of their manner of living, and can never be sure of death without ills or infirmity.

Therefore, the only mode of living that will render you secure in the hope of long years in health consists in your adopting, at least after the age of forty, the temperate life. This is not difficult to observe; since so many in the past, as history informs us, have observed it; and many, of whom I am one, are doing so at the present time—and we are all men; and man, being a rational animal, does much as he wills to do. The orderly and temperate life consists solely in the observance of two rules relative to the quality and the quantity of our food. The first, which regards quality, consists in our eating and drinking only such things as agree with the stomach; while the latter, which relates to quantity, consists in our using only such an amount of them as can be easily digested. Every man, by the time he has reached the age of forty, fifty, or, at any rate, sixty years, ought surely to be familiar with the conditions relating to the quality and quantity of food suited to his individual constitution; and he who observes these two rules, lives the orderly and temperate life— a life which has so much virtue and power that it renders the humors of the body most perfect, harmonious, and united. Indeed, they are brought to so satisfactory a condition that it is impossible they should ever be disturbed or altered by any form of disorder which we may incur, such as suffering extreme heat or cold, extraordinary fatigue, loss of customary sleep, or any other disorder—unless carried to the last excess.

In a word, the humors of the body, if it be governed by these two excellent rules relative to eating and drinking, resist weakening changes; thus fever, from which proceeds untimely death, is made impossible. It would seem, then, that every man should observe the orderly life; for it is beyond doubt that whoever does not follow it, but lives a disorderly and intemperate life, is, on account of excessive eating and drinking as well as of each and every one of the other innumerable disorders, constantly exposed to the danger of sickness and of death.

I admit it to be quite true that even those who are faithful to the two rules in regard to eating and drinking, —the observance of which constitutes the orderly and temperate life,—may, if exposed to some of the other disorders, be ailing for a day or two; but their indisposition will never be able to cause fever. They may, likewise, be influenced by the revolutions of the heavens. But neither the heavens, nor those disorders, are capable of disturbing the humors of those who follow the temperate life. This statement is but conformable to reason and nature; since the disorders of eating and drinking are internal, while all others are external only.

But there are persons, who, notwithstanding they are advanced in years, are none the less sensual. These maintain that neither the quantity nor the quality of their food or drink in any way injures them; therefore they use, without discrimination, large quantities of different viands, and are equally indiscreet with regard to drink, as if ignorant in what region of the body the stomach is situated. Thus they give proof of their gross sensuality and of the fact that they are the friends of gluttony. To these be it set forth, that what they assert is not possible according to nature; for whoever is born must, necessarily, bring into this world with him either a warm, or a cold, or else a moderate temperament. Now to say that warm foods agree with a warm temperament, that cold foods agree with a cold one, or that foods which are not of a moderate quality agree with a moderate temperament, is to state something naturally impossible. Therefore each one must choose the quality of food best suited to his constitution. Nor can those addicted to sensuality argue that, whenever they fall sick, they are enabled to free themselves of their sickness by clearing their systems with medicines and then observing a strict diet. It is very evident, thereby, that their trouble arises solely from indulgence in overmuch food, and that of a quality unsuited to their stomachs.

There are other persons, likewise elderly, who declare that they are obliged to eat and drink a great deal to maintain the natural warmth of their bodies, which constantly diminishes as their years increase; that they must have whatever food pleases their taste, whether hot, or cold, or temperate; and that, were they to live the temperate life, they would soon die. My answer thereto is that kind Mother Nature, in order that the agéd, whom she loves, may be preserved to yet greater age, has so provided that they are able to live with very little food, even as I do; because the stomachs of the old and feeble cannot digest large quantities. They need not fear that their lives will be shortened by reason of their not taking much food; since, by using very little when sick, they recover their health—and we know how sparing is the diet by the use of which invalids are restored. If, by confining themselves to a scanty fare when ill, they are freed of their disorders, why should they fear that, while using the larger quantity of food permitted by the temperate life, they should not be able to sustain their lives when in perfect health?

Others, again, say that it is better to suffer three or four times a year with their usual complaints, such as the gout, pains in the side, or other ills, rather than suffer the whole year round by not gratifying the appetite in the eating of those things which please the palate; since they know that by the medicine of a simple diet they can speedily recover. To them I reply that, with the increase of years and the consequent decrease of natural heat, dieting cannot always have sufficient power to undo the grave harm done by overeating. Hence they will necessarily succumb, at last, to these ailments of theirs: for sickness shortens life, even as health prolongs it.

Others, again, insist that it is far better to live ten years less, rather than to deprive one's self of the pleasure of gratifying the appetite. To this, I would say that men endowed with fine talents ought to prize a long life very highly. For the balance, it matters little that they do not value it; and, as they only make the world less beautiful, it is as well, perhaps, that they should die.

The great misfortune is that a refined and talented man should die before he has attained the natural limit of his life; since, if he is already a cardinal, when he has passed the age of eighty he will the more likely become pope; if he is a public official, how much greater is the possibility of his being called to the highest dignity in the state; if a man of letters, he will be looked upon as a god on earth; and the same is true of all others, according to their various occupations.

There are others, again, who, having come to old age, when the stomach naturally possesses less digestive power, will not consent to diminish the quantity of their food; nay, on the contrary, they increase it. And since, eating twice in the day, they find they cannot digest the great amount of food with which they burden their stomachs, they decide that it is better to eat but once; for, relying upon the long interval thus allowed between meals, they believe themselves able to eat, at one time, the same quantity which they had previously divided into two meals. But, in doing this, they are guilty of a fatal error; for they eat such a quantity that the stomach is overloaded so grievously as to suffer and become sour, converting the excessive food into those bad humors which kill men before their time.

I may say I have never known any person to live to a great age who indulged in that habit of life. Yet, all these persons would live to enjoy the blessings of extreme old age, if, as their years increase, they were but to reduce the quantity of their food and distribute it into several meals during the day, eating but little at a time; for the stomachs of the aged cannot digest a great quantity of food. Thus it is that an old man becomes, in regard to his nourishment, more and more like a child, who has to eat many times during the day.

Finally, we have those who say that while the temperate life may indeed be able to preserve a man in health, it cannot prolong his life. To these I answer that experience proves the contrary to be true; for we know of many persons, who, in times past, have prolonged their lives in this manner, and it may be observed that I, too, have thus prolonged mine. It cannot, whatever may be said, be objected that sobriety shortens the life of man as sickness unquestionably does. Therefore it is more conducive to the preservation of the radical moisture that a man be always healthy than that he be often sick. Hence we may reasonably conclude that the holy temperate life is the true mother of health and of longevity.

O most blessed and holy Temperate Life, so profitable to man, and so helpful! Thou enablest him to prolong his life to ripe old age, wherein he becomes wise and hearkens to reason,—that faculty which is man's peculiar property,—by means of which he is freed from sensuality, reason's worst enemy, and its bitter fruits, the passions and anxieties of the mind. Thou deliverest him also from the fearful thought of death. Oh, how much am I, thy faithful follower, indebted to thee! for it is through thee I enjoy this beautiful world—beautiful, indeed, to him who knows how, by thy effectual help, to make it so for himself, as thou hast enabled me to do!

At no other period of my existence, even in my sensual and disorderly youth, could I make life so beautiful; and yet, in order to enjoy every portion of it, I spared neither expense nor anything else. For I found that the pleasures of those years were, after all, but vain and filled with disappointments; so that I may say I never knew the world was beautiful until I reached old age.

O truly Happy Life! Thou, besides all the aforesaid manifold blessings thou grantest to thy old disciple, hast brought his stomach to so good and perfect a condition that he now relishes plain bread more than he ever did the most delicate viands in the years of his youth. All this thou dost because thou art reasonable, knowing that bread is the proper food of man when accompanied by a healthful appetite. This natural company, so long as a man follows the temperate life, he may be sure will never fail him; since, he eating but little, the stomach is but lightly burdened and has always, within a short time, a renewed desire for food. For this reason plain bread is so much relished. This I have proved by my own experience to be true; and I declare that I enjoy bread so much that I should be afraid of incurring the vice of gluttony, were it not that I am convinced it is necessary we should eat of it and that we cannot partake of a more natural food.

And thou, Mother Nature, so loving to thy old man, preserving him so long! Thou, besides providing that with little food he may maintain himself, hast moreover shown him—to favor him more and in order that his nourishment may be more profitable to him—that, while in youth he partook of two meals a day, now, that he has attained old age, his food must be divided into four; since, thus divided, it will be more easily digested by his stomach. In this way thou showest him that, as in youth he enjoyed the pleasures of the table but twice a day, now, in his old age, he may enjoy them four times, provided, however, he diminishes the quantity of his food as he advances in age.

As thou showest me, so do I observe. In consequence of which, my spirits, never oppressed by much food, but simply sustained, are always cheerful; and their energy is never greater than after meals. For I feel, when I leave the table, that I must sing, and, after singing, that I must write. This writing immediately after eating does not cause me any discomfort; nor is my mind less clear then than at other times. And I do not feel like sleeping; for the small amount of food I take cannot make me drowsy, as it is insufficient to send fumes from the stomach to the head.

Oh, how profitable it is to the old to eat but little! I, accordingly, who am filled with the knowledge of this truth, eat only what is enough to sustain my life; and my food is as follows:

First, bread; then, bread soup or light broth with an egg, or some other nice little dish of this kind; of meats, I eat veal, kid, and mutton; I eat fowls of all kinds, as well as partridges and birds like the thrush. I also partake of such salt-water fish as the goldney and the like; and, among the various fresh-water kinds, the pike and others.

As all these articles of food are suited to old people, the latter must be satisfied with them and not demand others; for they are quite sufficient, both in number and variety. Old persons, who, on account of poverty, cannot afford to indulge in all of these things, may maintain their lives with bread, bread soup, and eggs—foods that certainly cannot be wanting even to a poor man, unless he be one of the kind commonly known as good-for-nothing.

Yet, even though the poor should eat nothing but bread, bread soup, and eggs, they must not take a greater quantity than that which can be easily digested; for they must, at all times, remember that he who is constantly faithful to the above-mentioned rules in regard to the quantity and quality of his food, cannot die except by simple dissolution and without illness.

Oh, what a difference there is between the orderly and a disorderly life! The former blesses a man with perfect health and, at the same time, lengthens his life; while the latter, on the other hand, after bringing infirmities upon him, causes him to die before his time.

O thou unhappy and wretched disorderly life, thou art my sworn enemy; for thou knowest how to do nothing save to murder those who follow thee! How many of my dearest relatives and friends hast thou snatched from me, because, for thy sake, they would not listen to my advice! But for thee, I might at this moment be enjoying them!

Yet thou hast not succeeded in destroying me, though right willingly wouldst thou have done so; but, in spite of thee, I am still living and have reached this advanced age. I rejoice in my eleven grandchildren by whom I am surrounded, and who are all of bright intellect and noble nature, healthy, beautiful, fond of their studies, and inclined to good habits. Them, if I had listened to thee, I should never have enjoyed. Nor, had I followed thee, should I ever have experienced the pleasure now afforded me in the comfortable and beautiful habitations of my own creation, which I have surrounded with attractive gardens that have required great length of time to be brought to their present state of perfection.

No! for thy nature is to murder all those who follow thee, before they have the joy of witnessing the completion of their houses and gardens. Whilst I, to thy confusion, have already enjoyed the comfort of mine for many years.

Thou art a vice so pestilential that thou spreadest sickness and corruption throughout the world; for which reason I have determined to use every means in my power to deliver mankind from thy clutches, at least as far as I am able. I have resolved to work against thee in such a manner that my eleven grandchildren, after me, shall make thee known for that most wretched and vicious thing thou really art—the mortal enemy of all men who are born.

I am astonished, indeed, that men gifted with fine intellect—for there are many such—and who have reached a high position either in literature or some other occupation, should not embrace and follow the temperate life, at least when they come to the age of fifty or sixty and are troubled with any of the above-mentioned disorders; for, by following the temperate life, they could easily deliver themselves from these ailments, which, later on, if allowed to make further progress, will become incurable I do not wonder so much that some young men—those of them, at least, whose lives and habits are controlled by sensuality—should neglect sobriety; but certainly, after a man has passed the age of fifty, his life should be altogether guided by reason, which teaches that the gratification of the tastes and appetites means infirmity and death.

If this pleasure of the taste were a lasting one, we might have some patience with those who are so ready to yield to it. But it is so short-lived that it is no sooner begun than ended; while the infirmities which proceed from it are of very long duration. Moreover, to the man who follows the temperate life it is assuredly a great satisfaction to know, when he has finished eating, that the food he has taken will never cause him any sickness, but will keep him in perfect health.

I have now completed the short addition I wished to make to my treatise, "The Temperate Life"—an addition based on new arguments, though, at the same time, it is one of few words. For I have observed that long discourses are read by a few only, while brief ones are read by many; and I most heartily desire that this be read by many, in order that it may prove useful to many.

THE THIRD DISCOURSE

WRITTEN AT THE AGE OF NINETY-ONE

A LETTER FROM THE VENERABLE CORNARO

TO

THE REVEREND DANIEL BARBARO *

PATRIARCH ELECT OF AQUILEIA **

In which he gives mankind a rule of life that will, if
followed, assure a healthy and
happy old age

THE intellect of man truly partakes, in some degree,
of the divine prerogatives; for it was, indeed,
something divine which led him to find a way of
conversing, by means of writing, with another who is at
a distance. And a thing altogether divine, also, is that
natural faculty which enables him, when thus separated,
to behold, with the eye of thought, his beloved friend;
even as I now see you, Sir, and address to you this my
discourse on a pleasant and profitable subject.

* See Note J   ** See Note K

It is true that what I shall write will be upon a matter which has already been treated at other times, but never by any man at the age of ninety-one—at which time of life I am now writing On account of my age, I cannot be at fault; for the more my years multiply, the more my strength also increases And I, who am well aware from what cause this proceeds, feel compelled to make it known, and to show that all mankind may possess an earthly paradise after the age of eighty—a paradise with which I myself am blessed. But one cannot attain it otherwise than by means of holy self-restraint and the temperate life—two virtues much loved by the great God, because they are the enemies of sensuality and the friends of reason.

Now, Sir, to begin my discourse, I shall tell you that I have, within the past few days, been visited by a number of excellent professors who lecture in our University—doctors of medicine as well as philosophy. These gentlemen are all well acquainted with my age, and with my manner and habits of living, and know how full I am of cheerfulness and health. They know, too, that all my senses are in perfect condition—as also are my memory, my heart, and my mind—and that this is equally true of even my voice and my teeth. Nor are they ignorant of the fact that I constantly write, and with my own hand, eight hours a day, and always on subjects profitable to the world; and, in addition to this, that I walk and sing for many other hours.

Oh, how beautiful and sonorous has my voice become! If you could but hear me sing my prayers to the accompaniment of the lyre, as King David sang to that of the harp, I assure you that you would derive great pleasure.

Among other things, my visitors, the doctors, said:

"It is certainly marvelous that you are able to write so much, and upon subjects which require such thought and spirit." Concerning which, Sir, to tell you the truth, one can form no idea of the extreme pleasure and satisfaction I experience in writing thus; and, when I reflect that my writings will assuredly be useful to mankind, you can readily understand how great is my delight.

In fine, they said that I could by no means be considered an old man. For all my actions are those of youth, and not at all like the actions of other old persons; who, when they have arrived at the age of eighty, are almost helpless, besides having to suffer either from pains in the side or from some other complaint. In order to rid themselves of these troubles, they are continually subject to medical treatment or surgical operations, all of which are a great annoyance. Should there be any among them so fortunate as not to suffer from these infirmities, it will be found that their senses have begun to fail—either that of sight, or that of hearing, or some other one. We know of old persons who cannot walk, and of others who cannot use their hands because they tremble; and, if one of the number is so favored as to be free from the above troubles, it will be observed that he does not have a perfect memory, or else that his heart or his mind is weak. In a word, there is not one among them who enjoys a cheerful, happy, and contented life, such as mine is.

But, besides these many advantages which I possess, there is a special one which caused them to wonder extremely, because it is so very uncommon and contrary to nature; and that is, that I should have been able to keep myself alive during the past fifty years, notwithstanding the presence of an extreme difficulty—one of a mortal character—that has always been present in me.

[93]

This difficulty, which cannot be remedied, because it is a natural and hidden property of my constitution, consists in this: every year, from the beginning of July and throughout the whole of August, I cannot drink any kind of wine soever, be it of what variety of grape or of what country it may; for, during the whole of those two months, wine, besides being very unfriendly to my palate, disagrees with my stomach. So that, being without my milk,—for wine is truly the milk of the aged,— I am left without anything to drink; for waters, in whatever way they may be doctored or prepared, have not the virtue of wine, and fail to relieve me. My stomach becomes very much disordered, and I can eat but very little in consequence. This scarcity of food and lack of wine reduces me, by the latter part of August, to a condition of extreme mortal weakness. Neither does strong chicken broth nor any other remedy benefit me in the least; so that, through weakness alone,—not by any ailment,—I am brought very near a dying condition. It was evident to my visitors that, if the new wine, which I am always careful to have ready every year by the beginning of September, were not then forthcoming, the delay would be the cause of my death.

But they were yet more amazed at the fact that this new wine should have power to restore, in two or three days, the strength of which the old wine had deprived me—a thing of which they had themselves been eye-witnesses, and which could not be believed except by those who have seen it.

"Some of us," the doctors went on to say, "have observed your strange case for many years in succession; and, for the past ten years, it has been our opinion that, considering what a mortal difficulty you are under as well as your increasing age, it would be impossible for you to live more than a year or two longer. Yet we see, this year, that your weakness is less than in previous years.''

This blessing, associated with so many others, forced them to the conclusion that the union of all these many favors was a special grace bestowed on me at birth by Nature or by the heavens. In order to prove this conclusion true,—though as a matter of fact it is false, because not based upon good reasons and solid foundations, but simply upon their own opinions,—they found themselves under the necessity of giving utterance to many beautiful and lofty things with the finest eloquence. Eloquence, Sir, in men of intellect, verily has great power; so much so, indeed, that it will persuade some people to believe things that are not and can not be true. Their words, however, were to me a great pleasure and quite an amusing pastime; for it is certainly highly entertaining to listen to such talk from men of their intelligence.

And here I was granted another satisfaction; namely, the thought that advanced age, by reason of its experience, is able to confer learning upon the unlearned. This is not difficult to understand; for length of days is the real foundation of true knowledge—by means of which, alone, I was made aware of the erroneousness of their conclusions. Thus you see, Sir, how apt men are to err in forming their opinions when these are not based upon solid foundations.

In order, therefore, to undeceive them as well as to be of other service to them, I told them plainly that their conclusion was wrong, and that I would convince them of this by clearly proving that the blessing which I enjoy is not a special one, conferred upon me alone, but a general one and such as every man may possess if he choose. For I am only an ordinary mortal. Composed, like everybody else, of the four elements, I have—in addition to existence—sense, intellect, and reason. With the two latter faculties every one of us is born, the great God having willed that man, His creature whom He loves so well, should possess these gifts and blessings; for thus has He raised him above all the other creatures which have sense only, in order that, by means of these faculties, he may preserve himself in perfect health for many years. Therefore mine is a universal blessing, granted by God, and not by Nature or the heavens.

Man is, in his youth, however, more a sensual than a rational creature, and is inclined to live accordingly. Yet, when he has arrived at the age of forty or fifty, he certainly ought to realize that he has been enabled to reach the middle of life solely through the power of youth and a young stomach, those natural gifts which have helped him in the ascent of the hill. Now he must bear in mind that, burdened with the disadvantage of old age, he is about to descend it toward death And, since old age is exactly the opposite of youth, just as disorder is the reverse of order, it becomes imperative for him to change his habits of life with regard to eating and drinking, upon which a long and healthy life depends. As his earlier years were sensual and disorderly, the balance of them must be exactly the contrary, reasonable and orderly; because without order nothing can be preserved—least of all, the life of man. For it is well proved by experience that, while disorder does grievous harm, order is constantly beneficial.

It is necessarily impossible, in the nature of things, that a man should be determined to satisfy his taste and appetite, and yet, at the same time, commit no excesses; so, to be free from these excesses, I adopted the orderly and temperate life when I had once reached the state of manhood. I shall not deny that, in the beginning, I experienced some difficulty in abandoning an intemperate life after leading it for so many years. But, in order that I might be able to follow the temperate life, I prayed to God that He would grant me the virtue of self-restraint, knowing well that, when a man has firmly resolved to realize a noble enterprise and one which he is convinced he can accomplish,—though not without difficulty,—it is made much easier by bending all his energy upon doing it and actually setting to work. Spurred by this resolve, I began, little by little, to draw myself away from my disorderly life, and, little by little, to embrace the orderly one. In this manner I gave myself up to the temperate life, which has not since been wearisome to me; although, on account of the weakness of my constitution, I was compelled to be extremely careful with regard to the quality and quantity of my food and drink.

However, those persons who are blessed with strong constitutions may make use of many other kinds and qualities of food and drink, and partake of them in greater quantities, than I do; so that, even though the life they follow be the temperate one, it need not be as strict as mine, but much freer.

After they had heard my arguments and found them grounded, as they were, upon solid foundations, my visitors admitted that all I had said was true. The youngest of them, however, while ready to grant that the graces and advantages which I enjoyed were general, contended that I had had at least one special blessing vouchsafed me, in being able to relinquish so easily the kind of life I had so long followed, and to accustom myself to lead the other; because, although he had found this change, by his own experience, to be feasible, to him it had been very difficult.

I replied that, being a man like himself, I had also found it no easy matter to pass from the one kind of life to the other; but I knew it was unworthy of a man to abandon a noble undertaking simply on account of the difficulties encountered. For, the more obstacles a man meets and overcomes, the greater is the honor he gains and the more pleasing his action in the sight of God.

Our Maker, having ordained that the life of man should last for many years, is desirous that everyone should attain the extreme limit; since He knows that, after the age of eighty, man is wholly freed from the bitter fruits of sensuality and is replenished with those of holy reason. Then, of necessity, vices and sins are left behind. Wherefore it is that God wishes we should all live to extreme age; and He has ordained that they who do so reach their natural limit of earthly existence, shall terminate it without pain or sickness and by simple dissolution. Such is, indeed, the natural way of departing from this world, when we leave the mortal life to enter upon the immortal one—as it will be my lot to do; for I feel certain that I shall die while singing my prayers.

The awful thought of death does not trouble me in the least, although I realize, on account of my many years, I am nigh to it; for I reflect that I was born to die, and that many others have departed this life at a much younger age than mine.

Nor am I disturbed by that other thought, a companion of the foregoing one; namely, the thought of the punishment, which, after death, must be suffered for sins committed in this life. For I am a good Christian; and, as such, I am bound to believe that I shall be delivered from that punishment by virtue of the most sacred blood of Christ, which He shed in order to free us, His faithful servants, from those pains. Oh, what a beautiful life is mine, and how happy my end will be!

Having heard me out, the young man replied that, in order to gain the numerous and great advantages I had gained, he was determined to embrace the temperate life I had so long practiced He further declared he had already gained a highly important one; namely, that as he had always had a lively wish to live to a very great age, so now he desired to attain it as quickly as possible, in order to enter sooner into possession of the delights of that most enjoyable season.

The great longing I had to converse with you, Reverend Sir, has forced me to write at considerable length, while that which I still wish to say to you obliges me to continue my letter. But I shall be brief.

Dear Sir, there are some very sensual men who claim that I have only wasted time, as well as labor, in composing my treatise, "The Temperate Life," and the additions I have made to it; for, as they allege, I am exhorting men to adopt habits to which it is impossible for them to conform. They assert that my treatise will be as vain as is the "Republic" by Plato, who labored to write of a system which was impracticable—that, as his work is useless, so also will mine be.

I wonder much at such a line of argument on the part of intelligent men; for, if they have read my treatise, they must have clearly seen that I had led the temperate life for many years before writing anything regarding it. Nor should I ever have written, had not my own experience convinced me, without a shadow of doubt, not only that it is a practicable life and such as all men may easily lead, but, furthermore, that it profits

[99]

greatly because it is a life of virtue. I am so much indebted to it myself that I felt obliged to write of it, in order that I might make it known to others as the inestimable blessing it truly is. I know of many persons, who, after reading my treatise, have adopted that life; and I know, too, that in past ages, as we read in history, there were many who were remarkable as its followers. Hence the objection which is urged against Plato's "Republic" certainly does not hold good in the case of my treatise, "The Temperate Life." But these sensual men, enemies of reason and friends of intemperance, will only receive their just deserts if, while seeking to gratify their every taste and appetite, they incur painful sicknesses, and meet, as many such do, with a premature death.

LORD BACON
1561—1626

From the painting by Paul Van Somer—No. 520. National Portrait Gallery,
London

THE FOURTH DISCOURSE

WRITTEN AT THE AGE OF NINETY-FIVE

THE BIRTH AND DEATH OF MAN

A LOVING EXHORTATION

In which, by the authority of his own experience, the aged author
strives to persuade all mankind to follow the orderly and
temperate life, in order that they, too, may reach an
advanced age, in which to enjoy all those graces
and blessings that God in His goodness
is pleased to grant to mortals

IN order that I may not fail in the discharge of my
'duty—a law to which every man is bound—and, at
the same time, that I may not forego the pleasure
I invariably experience in being of service to my
fellow-men, I have determined to write and to make
known to those persons who do not know them—because
unacquainted with me—the things which are known and
seen by those who frequent my company. Certain facts
I shall now relate will, to some, appear difficult of belief

and well-nigh impossible; nevertheless, since they are all
true and to be seen in reality, I will not refrain from
writing of them, that the knowledge of them may benefit
the world at large.

In the first place, I shall say that I have, through
the mercy of God, reached the age of ninety-five; that I
find myself, in spite of my great age, healthy, strong,
contented, and happy; and that I continually praise the
Divine Majesty for so much favor conferred upon me.
Moreover, in the generality of other old men whom I see,
no sooner have they arrived at the age of seventy, than
they are ailing and devoid of strength; melancholy; and
continually occupied with the thought of death. They
fear, from day to day, that their last hour will come; so
much so, that it is impossible for anything to relieve
their minds of that dread For my part, I do not experience the least trouble at the idea of death; for, as I
shall later on explain more clearly, I cannot bring myself to give it so much as a thought.

In addition to this, I shall demonstrate, beyond
question, the certainty I entertain of living to the age of
one hundred years. But, in order that I may proceed
methodically, I shall begin with the consideration of man
at his birth, studying him thence, step by step, through
every stage of life until his death.

I say, then, that some human beings are ushered into
this world with so little vitality that they live but a very
few days, months, or years, as the case may be. The
cause of this want of vitality it is impossible to know to
a certainty, whether it arises from some imperfection of
the father or mother, from the revolutions of the heavens,
or from some defect in Nature. This latter, however,
can happen only when she is subject to the influence of
the heavens; for I could never persuade myself to believe

that Nature, being the mother of all, could be so ungenerous to any of her children. Hence, not being able to ascertain the real cause, we must be content to accept the facts as we daily observe them.

Others are born with greater vitality, yet with feeble and poor constitutions. Of these, some live to the age of ten, others to twenty, others even to thirty or forty years; but they never reach old age.

Others, again, begin life with perfect constitutions and live to old age; but the health of the greater part of them is, as I have said before, in a very wretched condition. They are themselves the sole cause of this; simply because, foolishly relying too much upon their perfect natures, they are unwilling, under any circumstances, to modify their manner of living when passing from youth to old age, as though they still possessed their early vigor unimpaired. Indeed, they expect to be able to continue to live as disorderly a life, after they have begun the descent of the hill, as they did throughout the years of their youth; since they never for a moment consider that they are approaching old age and that their constitutions have lost their former vigor. Nor do they ever pause to reflect that their stomachs have lost their natural heat, and that they should, by reason of this circumstance, be more careful with regard to quality in the selection of their food and drink, and also with regard to the quantity thereof, to lessen it gradually. But the latter they refuse to do; instead of which, they attempt to augment it, claiming—as an excuse—that, since a man loses his strength with advancing age, the deficiency must be made good by a greater quantity of nourishment, as it is that which keeps him alive.

These persons, however, argue very incorrectly. For, as the natural heat of man gradually diminishes with the increase of age, it becomes necessary for him to decrease gradually, in proportion, the amount of his food and drink; since nature requires very little to maintain the life of an old man. Although reason should convince them that this is the case, yet these men refuse to admit it, and pursue their usual life of disorder as heretofore. Were they to act differently, abandoning their irregular habits and adopting orderly and temperate ones, they would live to old age—as I have—in good condition. Being, by the grace of God, of so robust and perfect constitutions, they would live until they reached the age of a hundred and twenty, as history points out to us that others—born, of course, with perfect constitutions—have done, who led the temperate life.

I am certain I, too, should live to that age, had it been my good fortune to receive a similar blessing at my birth; but, because I was born with a poor constitution, I fear I shall not live much beyond a hundred years. Yet all those who are born delicate, like myself, would no doubt reach, in perfect health, the age of a hundred and more years,—as I feel will be the case with me,—were they to embrace the temperate life as I have done.

This certainty of being able to live for many years seems to me of great value. Indeed, it should be highly prized; since no man can be sure of even one single hour of existence unless he be one of those who follow the temperate life. These alone have solid ground for their hopes of a long life—hopes founded upon good and true natural reasons which have never been known to fail. For it is impossible, in the regular course of nature, that he who leads the orderly and temperate life should ever fall sick; nor, though death is eventually certain, need he ever die a premature or an unnatural death. It is not possible that he should die earlier than is occasioned by the natural failure of the body; for the temperate life has the power to remove every cause of sickness; and without a cause, sickness cannot develop. When the cause is removed, sickness likewise is removed; and sickness being removed, an unnatural death is out of the question.

It is beyond doubt that the orderly and temperate life has the power and strength to remove the causes of illness; for it is that which changes, for the better, the humors of the body upon which—according as they are good or bad—man's health or sickness, life or death, depends. If these humors were bad, the temperate life has the natural power to make them better and, in time, perfect; and, being able to make them so, it has the further power to maintain, equalize, and unite them so that they cannot become separated, agitated, or altered, and cause cruel fevers and, finally, death.

It is true, however,—and this no one can reasonably deny,—that even though they be made ever so good, yet, as time progresses, consuming all things, these humors of the body will also be consumed and dissolved at last. When they are thus dissolved, man must die a natural death,—without pain or illness,—just as, in the course of time, I shall pass away when the humors of my body shall be finally consumed.

They are now, however, all in good condition. It is not possible they should be otherwise; for I am healthy, cheerful, and contented; my appetite is so good that I always eat with relish; my sleep is sweet and peaceful; and, moreover, all my faculties are in a condition as perfect as ever they were; my mind is more than ever keen and clear; my judgment sound; my memory tenacious; my heart full of life; and my voice—that which is wont to be the first thing in man to fail—is so strong and sonorous that, in consequence, I am obliged to sing aloud my morning and evening prayers, which I had formerly been accustomed to say in a low and hushed tone. These are true and certain indications that the humors of my body are all good and can never be consumed save by time alone, as everybody who is well acquainted with me declares.

Oh, how glorious will have been this life of mine! so full of all the happiness that can be enjoyed in this world, and so free—as it truly is—from the tyranny of sensuality, which, thanks to my many years, has been driven out by reason! For, where reason reigns, no place is left for sensuality, nor for its bitter fruits, the passions and anxieties of the mind accompanied by a well-nigh endless train of afflicting and sorrowful thoughts.

As for the thought of death, it can have no place in my mind; for there is nothing sensual in me. Even the death of any of my grandchildren, or of any other relatives or friends, could never cause me trouble except the first instinctive motion of the soul, which, however, soon passes away. How much less could I lose my serenity through any loss of worldly wealth! Many of my friends have witnessed this to their great astonishment. However, this is the privilege of those only who attain extreme age by means of the temperate life and not merely through the aid of a strong constitution; it is the former, not the latter, who enjoy every moment of life, as I do, amid continual consolations and pleasures.

And who would not enjoy life at an age when, as I have already shown, it is free from the innumerable miseries by which we all know the younger ages are afflicted! How wholly mine, in its happiness, is free from these miseries, I shall now set forth.

To begin, the first of joys is to be of service to one's beloved country. Oh, what a glorious enjoyment it is, what a source of infinite pleasure to me, that I am able to show Venice the manner in which she may preserve her valuable lagoon and harbor so that they will not alter for thousands of years to come! Thus she will continue to bear her wonderful and magnificent name of Virgin City, which indeed she is, there being no other like her in all the world; while her high and noble title, Queen of the Sea, will, by this means, become still more exalted. I can never fail to fully rejoice and take great comfort in this.

There is another thing which affords me much contentment; it is, that I have shown this Virgin and Queen how she may be abundantly supplied with food, by preparing for cultivation—with returns much above the expense—large tracts of land, marshes as well as dry plains, all hitherto useless and waste.

Another sweet and unalloyed satisfaction I experience is, that I have pointed out to Venice how she may be made stronger, although she is now so strong as to be almost impregnable; how her loveliness may be increased, although she is now so beautiful; how she may be made richer, although now exceedingly wealthy; and how her air, which is now so good, may be made perfect.

These three pleasures afford me the greatest possible satisfaction, because based wholly upon my desire to be useful to others. And who could find a drawback to them, since in reality none exists!

Having lost a considerable portion of my income through misfortunes befallen my grandchildren, it is another source of happiness to me that, merely through the activity of my thoughts which do not sleep, without any bodily fatigue, and with but little labor of the mind, I found a sure and unerring way of repairing—yea, of doubly remedying—that loss, by means of true and scientific farming.

Yet one more gratification afforded me is the abundant evidence I receive that my treatise, "The Temperate Life," which I composed to be of service to others, is really doing much good. I can entertain no doubt of this; since some tell me, by word of mouth, that they have derived great benefit from it—and it is evident they have; while others acknowledge by letter that, after God, it is to me they owe their very lives.

Another great consolation enjoyed by me is that of writing with my own hand—and, to be of use, I write a great deal—on various topics, especially upon architecture and agriculture.

Yet another of my pleasures consists in having the good fortune to converse with various men of fine and high intellect, from whom, even at my advanced age, I never fail to learn something. Oh, what a delight it is to feel that, at this great age of mine, it is no labor whatsoever to learn, no matter how great, high, and difficult the subjects may be!

Furthermore, though it is a thing which to some may seem impossible and in no manner to be believed, I wish to say that, in this extreme age of mine, I enjoy two lives at the same time: one, the earthly, which I possess in reality; the other, the heavenly, which I possess in thought. For thought truly has the power of imparting happiness when it is grounded upon something we are confident we shall enjoy, as I do firmly hope and certainly believe I shall enjoy an eternal life through the infinite goodness and mercy of the great God. I enjoy this earthly existence through the excellence of the orderly and temperate life, which is so pleasing to His Majesty because it is full of virtue and the enemy of vice. At the same time I rejoice in the heavenly one, which God has given me now to enjoy in thought; for He has taken from me the power to think of it differently, so sure am I to possess it some day.

And I hold that our departure from this world is not death, but merely a passage which the soul makes from this earthly life to the heavenly one, immortal and infinitely perfect—a belief which I am sure cannot but be the true one.

Hence my thoughts are raised to heights so sublime that they cannot descend to the consideration of such worldly and common occurrences as the death of the body, but, rather, are wholly absorbed in living the heavenly and divine life In this manner it comes to pass that, as I said before, I incessantly enjoy two lives. And I shall not feel any regret on account of the great happiness I have in this earthly life, when that life shall cease; for then my joy will be boundless, knowing, as I do, that the ending of this life is but the beginning of another, glorious and immortal.

Who could ever find weariness in a lot so truly blessed and happy as the one I enjoy! Yet this happiness would be the portion of every man if he would but lead a life similar to the one I have led. And, assuredly, it is in every man's power to lead such a life; for I am nothing but a man and not a saint, only a servant of God, to Whom the orderly life is well-pleasing.

There are many men who embrace a holy and beautiful, spiritual and contemplative life, full of prayer. Oh, were they faithful followers also of the orderly and temperate life, how much more pleasing in the sight of God would they render themselves, and how much more beautiful would they make the world! They would be esteemed as highly as were those, who, in ancient times, added the practice of the temperate life to that of the spiritual.

[111]

Like them, they would live to the age of one hundred and twenty; and, by the power of God, they would perform countless miracles, just as those others did. Furthermore, they would constantly enjoy a healthy, happy, and cheerful life; whereas they are at present, for the greater part, unhealthy, melancholy, and dissatisfied.

Since some of them believe that these afflictions are sent them by the great God for their salvation,—that they may, in this life, make reparation for their sins,—I cannot refrain from saying that, according to my judgment, these persons are mistaken; for I cannot believe God deems it good that man, whom He so much loves, should be sickly, melancholy, and discontented. I believe, on the contrary, that He wishes him to be healthy, cheerful, and contented, precisely as those holy men in ancient times were; who, becoming ever better servants of His Majesty, performed the many and beautiful miracles of which we read.

Oh, what a lovely and enjoyable place this world would be—even more so than it was in the olden times! For there are now many Orders which then did not exist, in which, if the temperate life were followed, we might see so many venerable old men; and a wonderful sight it would be. Nor would they, in the practice of the temperate life, deviate from the regular rules of living enjoined by their Orders; on the contrary, they would improve upon them. For every Order allows its members, in the way of fare, to eat bread and drink wine, and, in addition to that, sometimes to take eggs. Some Orders allow even meat, besides vegetable soups, salads, fruits, and pastries made with eggs—foods which often harm them, and to some are a cause of death. They make use of these because allowed to do so by their Orders, thinking, perhaps, they would be doing wrong were they to abstain from them. But it would not be wrong at all; indeed, they would act more properly, if, after they have passed the age of thirty, they were to give up the use of such foods, and live solely upon bread dipped in wine, bread soup, and eggs with bread—the true diet to preserve the life of a man of poor constitution   It would be, after all, a rule less severe than that of those holy men of old in the deserts; who, subsisting entirely upon wild fruits and roots of herbs, and drinking nothing but pure water, lived, as I have said, many years, and were always healthy, cheerful, and contented.   So, also, would these of our own day be, were they to follow the temperate life. And, at the same time, they would more easily find the way to ascend to heaven, which is always open to every faithful Christian; for thus it was our Redeemer left it when He descended thence, coming upon earth that He might shed His precious blood to deliver us from the tyrannical servitude of the devil—all of which He did through His infinite goodness.

In conclusion, I wish to say that, since old age is—as, in truth, it is—filled and overflowing with so many graces and blessings, and since I am one of the number who enjoy them, I cannot fail—not wishing to be wanting in charity—to give testimony to the fact, and to fully certify to all men that my enjoyment is much greater than I can now express in writing.   I declare that I have no other motive for writing but my hope that the knowledge of so great a blessing as my old age has proved to be, will induce every human being to determine to adopt this praiseworthy orderly and temperate life, in favor of which I ceaselessly keep repeating, Live, live, that you may become better servants of God!

O Luxury! thou curst by Heaven's decree,
How ill exchang'd are things like these for thee!
How do thy potions, with insidious joy,
Diffuse their pleasures only to destroy!
Kingdoms by thee, to sickly greatness grown,
Boast of a florid vigor not their own
At every draught more large and large they grow,
A bloated mass of rank unwieldy woe;
Till sapp'd their strength, and every part unsound,
Down, down they sink, and spread a ruin round.

       —Oliver Goldsmith.

PART II

EXTRACTS

SELECTED AND ARRANGED FROM

LORD BACON'S

"HISTORY OF LIFE AND DEATH"

AND FROM

SIR WILLIAM TEMPLE'S

"HEALTH AND LONG LIFE"

The first physicians by debauch were made,
Excess began and sloth sustains the trade.
By chase our long-lived fathers earn'd their food;
Toil strung the nerves, and purified the blood;
But we their sons, a pamper'd race of men,
Are dwindled down to threescore years and ten.
Better to hunt in fields for health unbought
Than fee the doctor for a nauseous draught.
The wise for cure on exercise depend:
God never made his work for man to mend.

—John Dryden.

EXTRACTS

Selected and Arranged from

LORD BACON'S

"History of Life and Death"

Etc.*

To the Present Age, and Posterity. Greeting:

I have hope, and wish, that it [the "History of Life and Death"] may conduce to a common good; and that the nobler sort of physicians will advance their thoughts, and not employ their time wholly in the sordidness of cures; neither be honored for necessity only; but that they will become coadjutors and instruments of the Divine omnipotence and clemency in prolonging and renewing the life of man. For though we Christians do continually aspire and pant after the land

* See Note C

[117]

of promise, yet it will be a token of God's favor toward us in our journeyings through this world's wilderness, to have our shoes and garments—I mean those of our frail bodies—little worn or impaired.

FR. ST. ALBANS.

Men fear death, as children fear to go into the dark; and as that natural fear in children is increased with tales, so is the other. Certainly, the contemplation of death, as the wages of sin, and passage to another world, is holy and religious; but the fear of it, as a tribute due unto nature, is weak. It is as natural to die as to be born. He that dies in an earnest pursuit, is like one that is wounded in hot blood; who, for the time, scarce feels the hurt; and therefore a mind fixed and bent upon somewhat that is good, doth avert the dolors of death. It will be hard to know the ways of death, unless we search out and discover the seat or house, or rather den, of death.

Truth, which only doth judge itself, teacheth that the inquiry of truth, which is the love-making or wooing of it, the knowledge of truth, which is the presence of it, and the belief of truth, which is the enjoying of it, is the sovereign good of human nature. Certainly, it is heaven upon earth, to have a man's mind move in charity, rest in providence, and turn upon the poles of truth.

Man, the servant and interpreter of nature, does and understands as much as he has actually or mentally observed of the order of nature—himself, meanwhile, inclosed around by the laws of nature; he neither knows nor can do more. The limit, therefore, of human power and knowledge is in the faculties, with which man is endowed by nature for moving and perceiving, as well as in the state of present things. These faculties, though of themselves weak and inept, are yet capable, when properly and regularly managed, of setting before the judgment and use things most remote from sense and action, and of overcoming greater difficulty of works and obscurity of knowledge than any one hath yet learned to wish.

Men see clearly, like owls, in the night of their own notions; but, in experience, as in the daylight, they wink and are but half-sighted. I should wish to have Paracelsus and Severinus for criers, when, with such clamors, they convoke men to the suggestions of experience.

It appears to me that men know not either their acquirements or their powers, and trust too much to the former, and too little to the latter. Hence it arises, that, either estimating the arts they have become acquainted with at an absurd value, they require nothing more; or, forming too low an opinion of themselves, they waste their powers on trivial objects, without attempting anything to the purpose. The sciences have thus their own pillars, fixed as it were by fate; since men are not roused to penetrate beyond them either by zeal or hope. All sciences seem, even now, to flourish most in their first authors—Aristotle, Galen, Euclid, and Ptolemy; succession having not effected, nay, barely attempted, any great matter. Men, therefore, are to be admonished to rouse up their spirits, and try their strengths and turns, and not refer all to the opinions and brains of a few. Even those who have been determined to try for themselves, to add their support to learning, and to enlarge its limits, have not dared entirely to desert received opinions nor to seek the springhead of things. Yet there have not been wanting some, who, with greater daring, have considered everything open to them; and, employing the force of their wit, have opened a passage for themselves and their dogmas by prostrating and destroying all before them.

Power to do good is the true and lawful end of aspiring; for good thoughts—though God accept them—toward men are little better than good dreams, except they be put in act.

The greatest trust between man and man is the trust of giving counsel. Heraclitus saith well in one of his enigmas, "Dry light is ever the best"; and certain it is, that the light that a man receiveth by counsel from another, is drier and purer than that which cometh from his own understanding and judgment, which is ever infused and drenched in his affections and customs; so there is as much difference between the counsel that a friend giveth, and that a man giveth himself, as there is between the counsel of a friend and of a flatterer; for there is no such flatterer as is a man's self, and there is no such remedy against flattery of a man's self as the liberty of a friend. The best preservative to keep the mind in health is the faithful admonition of a friend. It is a strange thing to behold what gross errors and extreme absurdities many do commit, for want of a friend to tell them of them, to the great damage both of their fame and fortune.

The help of good counsel is that which setteth business straight. The wisest princes need not think it any diminution to their greatness, or derogation to their sufficiency, to rely upon counsel. Solomon hath pronounced that "in counsel is stability." Solomon's son found the force of counsel, as his father saw the necessity of it.

It hath been noted that those who ascribe openly too much to their own wisdom and policy, end unfortunate. He that questioneth much, shall learn much and content much—especially if he apply his questions to the skill of the persons whom he asketh; for he shall give them occasion to please themselves in speaking, and himself shall continually gather knowledge. Set before thee the best examples; for imitation is a globe of precepts. Ask counsel of both times: of the ancienter time what is best, and of the latter time what is fittest. Do not drive away such as bring thee information, as meddlers; but accept of them in good part. Always, when thou changest thine opinion or course, profess it plainly, and declare it, together with the reasons that move thee to change.

This is a true and grave admonition, that we expect not to receive things necessary for life and manners from philosophical abstractions, but from the discreet observation and experience, and the universal knowledge, of the things of this world. The shame it is, that men, having the use of so many arts, are not able to get unto themselves such things as nature itself bestows upon many other creatures! Whosoever doth thoroughly consider the nature of man, may be in a manner the contriver of his own fortune, and is born to command.

It is an ancient saying and complaint, that life is short and art long; wherefore it behooveth us, who make it our chiefest aim to perfect arts, to take upon us the consideration of prolonging man's life—God, the author of all truth and life, prospering our endeavors. Only the inquiry is difficult how to attain this blessing of long life, so often promised in the old law; and so much the rather, because it is corrupted with false opinions and vain reports. Verily, it were a great sin against the golden fortune of mankind, the pledge of empire, for me to turn aside to the pursuit of most fleeting shadows. One bright and radiant light of truth must be placed in the midst, which may illuminate the whole, and in a moment dispel all errors. Certain feeble and pale lamps are not to be carried round to the several corners and holes of errors and falsehoods.

We ingeniously profess that some of those things

which we shall propound, have not been tried by us by way of experiment,—for our course of life doth not permit that,—but are derived, as we suppose, upon good reasons, out of our principles and grounds,—of which some we set down, others we reserve in our mind,—and are, as it were, cut and digged out of the rock and mine of Nature herself. Nevertheless, we have been careful, and that with all providence and circumspection,—seeing the Scripture saith of the body of man, that it is more worth than raiment,—to propound such remedies as may at least be safe, if peradventure they be not fruitful.

All things in living creatures are in their youth repaired entirely; nay, they are for a time increased in quantity, bettered in quality, so as the matter of reparation might be eternal, if the manner of reparation did not fail. But this is the truth of it: there is in the declining of age an unequal reparation. By which it comes to pass, that, in process of time, the whole tends to dissolution; and even those very parts which, in their own nature, are with much ease reparable, yet, through the decay of the organs of reparation, can no more receive reparation, but decline, and in the end utterly fail. And the cause of the termination of life is this: the spirits, like a gentle flame, continually preying upon bodies, conspiring with the outward air,—which is ever sucking and drying of them,—do, in time, destroy the whole fabric of the body, as also the particular engines and organs thereof, and make them unable for the work of reparation. These are the true ways of natural death, well and faithfully to be revolved in our minds; for he that knows not the way of nature, how can he succor her or turn her about?

We see the reign or tyranny of custom, what it is Men's thoughts are much according to their inclination, their discourse and speeches according to their learning and infused opinions; but their deeds are after as they have been accustomed. Therefore, as Machiavel well noteth, there is no trusting to the force of nature, nor to the bravery of words, except it be corroborate by custom. Nature is often hidden, sometimes overcome, seldom extinguished. But custom, only, doth alter and subdue nature. He that seeketh victory over his nature, let him not set himself too great nor too small tasks; for the first will make him dejected by often failing, and the second will make him a small proceeder—though by often prevailing. Where nature is mighty and, therefore, the victory hard, the degrees had need be: first, to stay and arrest nature in time—like to him that would say over the four-and-twenty letters when he was angry; then, to go less in quantity—as if one should, in forbearing wine, come from drinking healths to a draught at a meal; and, lastly, to discontinue altogether; but if a man have the fortitude and resolution to enfranchise himself at once, that is the best. But let not a man trust his victory over his nature too far; for nature will lie buried a great time, and yet revive upon the occasion, or temptation; like as it was with Æsop's damsel, turned from a cat to a woman, who sat very demurely at the board's end till a mouse ran before her.

The predominancy of custom is everywhere visible; insomuch as a man would wonder to hear men profess, protest, engage, give great words, and then do just as they have done before, as if they were dead images and engines, moved only by the wheels of custom. A man's nature runs either to herbs or weeds; therefore let him seasonably water the one, and destroy the other. Neither is the ancient rule amiss, to bend nature as a wand to a contrary extreme, whereby to set it right; understanding it where the contrary extreme is no vice. Many examples may be put of the force of custom, both upon mind and body; therefore, since custom is the principal magistrate of man's life, let men by all means endeavor to obtain good customs. Certainly, custom is most perfect when it beginneth in young years; this we call education, which is, in effect, but an early custom.

To procure long life, the body of man must be considered. The ancients seemed not to despair of attaining the skill, by means and medicines, to put off old age, and to prolong life; but this to be numbered rather among such things, having been once happily attained unto, are now—through men's negligence and carelessness—utterly perished and lost, than among such as have been always denied and never granted; for they signify and show that the divine bounty is not wanting unto men in the obtaining of such gifts. Surely every medicine is an innovation; and he that will not apply new remedies must expect new evils; for time is the greatest innovator. And if time, of course, alter things to the worse, and wisdom and counsel shall not alter them to the better, what shall be the end?

The nature of the spirits is as the uppermost wheel, which turneth about the other wheels in the body of man; and, therefore, in the intention of long life, that ought to be first placed. Age is nothing of itself, being only the measure of time; that which causeth the effect is the native spirit of bodies, which sucketh up the moisture of the body, and then, together with it, flieth forth; and the air ambient, which multiplieth itself upon the native spirits and juices of the body, and preyeth upon them. The spirits are the master workmen of all effects in the body; this is manifest by consent, and by infinite instances. The actions or functions which are in the several members, follow the nature of the members themselves,—attraction, retention, digestion, assimilation, separation, excretion, perspiration, even sense itself,—

according to the propriety of the several organs; yet none of these actions would ever have been actuated, but by the vigor and presence of the vital spirit, and heat thereof. The operation upon the spirits, and their waxing green again, is the most ready and compendious way to long life.

It conduceth unto long life, and to the more placid motion of the spirits, which thereby do less prey and consume the juice of the body, either that men's actions be free and voluntary, or, on the other side, that their actions be full of regulation and commands within themselves; for then the victory and performing of the command giveth a good disposition to the spirits, especially if there be a proceeding from degree to degree; for then the sense of the victory is the greater. An example of the former of these is in a country life; and of the latter in monks and philosophers, and such as do continually enjoin themselves. The spirits, to keep the body fresh and green, are so to be wrought and tempered that they may be in substance dense, not rare; in heat strong, not eager; in quantity sufficient for the offices of life, not redundant or turgid; in motion appeased, not dancing or unequal. It is to be seen in flames, that the bigger they are, the stronger they break forth, and the more speedily they consume. And, therefore, overgreat plenty, or exuberance of the spirits, is altogether hurtful to long life; neither need one wish a greater store of spirits, than what is sufficient for the functions of life and the office of a good reparation.

The living spirit stands in need of three things that it may subsist: convenient motion, temperate refrigeration, and fit aliment. We suppose all things in moderation to be best.

No body can be healthy without exercise, neither natural body nor politic. It is altogether requisite to long life, that the body should never abide long in one posture; but that every half-hour, at least, it change the posture, saving only in sleep. As for exercise, an idle life doth manifestly make the flesh soft and dissipable; robust exercise, so it be without overmuch sweating or weariness, maketh it hard and compact. Also exercise within cold water, as swimming, is very good; and, generally, exercise abroad is better than that within houses Exercises which stir up a good strong motion, but not overswift, or to our utmost strength, do not hurt, but rather benefit.

Men ought to beware that they use not exercise and a spare diet both; but if much exercise, then a plentiful diet; and if sparing diet, then little exercise. The benefits that come of exercise are: first, that it sendeth nourishment into the parts more forcibly; secondly, that it helpeth to excern by sweat, and so maketh the parts assimilate the more perfectly; thirdly, that it maketh the substance of the body more solid and compact, and so less apt to be consumed and depredated by the spirits.

That exercise may resolve either the spirits or the juices as little as may be, it is necessary that it be used when the stomach is not altogether empty; and, therefore, that it may not be used upon a full stomach,—which doth much concern health,—nor yet upon an empty stomach,—which doth no less concern long life,—it is best to take a breakfast in the morning, of plain meat and drink; yet that very light, and in moderate quantity.

Both exercise and frications conduce much to long life; for agitation doth fineliest diffuse and commix things by small portions. But in exercise and frications there is the same reason and caution, that the body may not perspire or exhale too much. Therefore, exercise is better in the open air than in the house, and better in winter than in summer. Gentle frications, and moderate exercises, causing rather perspiration than sweating, conduce much to long life. But, generally, exercise, if it be much, is no friend to prolongation of life; which is one cause why women live longer than men, because they stir less.*

Refrigeration, or cooling of the body, which passeth some other ways than by the stomach, is useful for long life. The reason is at hand: for seeing a refrigeration not temperate, but powerful,—especially of the blood,—is above all things necessary to long life, this can by no means be effected from within as much as is requisite, without the destruction of the stomach and bowels.

The body of man doth regularly require renovation by aliment every day, and a body in health can scarce endure fasting three days together; notwithstanding, use and custom will do much, even in this case; but in sickness, fasting is less grievous to the body. We would have men rightly to observe and distinguish, that those things which are good for a healthful life, are not always good for a long life; for there are some things which do further the alacrity of the spirits, and the strength and vigor of the functions, which, notwithstanding, do cut off from the sum of life. It is hard to distinguish that which is generally held good and wholesome, from that which is good particularly, and fit for thine own body. It doth no good to have the aliment ready, in a degree removed, but to have it of that kind, and so prepared and supplied, that the spirit may work upon it; for the staff of a torch alone will not maintain the flame, unless it be fed with wax; neither can men live upon herbs alone. Nourishment ought to be of an inferior nature and more simple substances than the thing nourished. Plants are nourished with the earth and water, living creatures with plants, man with living creatures. There are also cer-

* See Note A

[127]

tain creatures feeding upon flesh; and man himself takes plants into a part of his nourishment.

The stomach—which, as they say, is the master of the house, and whose strength and goodness is fundamental to the other concoctions—ought so to be guarded and confirmed that it may be without intemperateness hot; it is to be kept ever in appetite, because appetite sharpens digestion. This also is most certain, that the brain is in some sort in the custody of the stomach; and, therefore, those things which comfort and strengthen the stomach, do help the brain by consent. I do verily conceive it good that the first draught be taken at supper, warm. I knew a physician that was very famous; who, in the beginning of dinner and supper, would usually eat a few spoonfuls of very warm broth with much greediness, and then would presently wish that it were out again, saying he had no need of the broth, but only of the warmth.

A pythagorical or monastical diet, according to strict rules, and always exactly equal,—as that of Cornaro was,—seemeth to be very effectual for long life. If there were anything eminent in the Spartans, that was to be imputed to the parsimony of their diet. It is not more true, that many dishes have caused many diseases,—as the proverb is,—than this is true, that many medicines have caused few cures.

It seems to be approved by experience, that a spare diet, and almost a pythagorical,—such as is either prescribed by the strict rules of a monastical life, or practiced by hermits, which have necessity and poverty for their rule,—rendereth a man long-lived. Celsus, who was not only a learned physician, but a wise man, is not to be omitted, who adviseth interchanging and alternation of the diet, but still with an inclination to the more benign. Conservation of health hath commonly need of no more than some short courses of physic; but length of life cannot be hoped without an orderly diet.

Curing of diseases is effected by temporary medicines; but lengthening of life requireth observation of diets. Those things which come by accident, as soon as the causes are removed, cease again; but the continual course of nature, like a running river, requires a continual rowing and sailing against the stream. Therefore we must work regularly by diets. Now, diets are of two kinds: set diets, which are to be observed at certain times; and familiar diet, which is to be admitted into our daily repast. But the set diets are the more potent; for those things which are of so great virtue that they are able to turn nature back again, are, for the most part, more strong, and more speedily altering, than those which may without danger be received into a continual use.

Certainly this is without all question: diet, well ordered, bears the greatest part in the prolongation of life. But if the diet shall not be altogether so rigorous and mortifying, yet, notwithstanding, shall be always equal and constant to itself, it worketh the same effect. We see it in flames, that a flame somewhat bigger—so it be always alike and quiet—consumeth less of the fuel, than a lesser flame blown with bellows, and by gusts stronger or weaker. That which the regimen and diet of Cornaro, the Venetian, showed plainly; who did eat and drink so many years together by a just weight, whereby he exceeded a hundred years of age, strong in limbs, and entire in his senses.

I am of opinion, that emaciating diseases, afterward well cured, have advanced many in the way of long life; for they yield new juice, the old being consumed; and to recover a sickness is to renew youth. Therefore it were good to make some artificial diseases, which is done by strict and emaciating diets.

We see that all things which are done by nutrition ask a long time; but those which are done by embracing of the like—as it is in infusions—require no long time. Therefore, alimentation from without would be of principal use; and so much the more, because the faculties of concoction decay in old age; so that if there could be some auxiliary nutritions, by bathing, unctions, or else by clysters, these things in conjunction might do much, which single are less available.

Also, sleep doth supply somewhat to nourishment; and, on the other side, exercise doth require it more abundantly. But as moderate sleep conferreth to long life, so much more if it be quiet and not disturbed.

Assimilation is best done when all local motion is suspended. The act itself of assimilation is chiefly accomplished in sleep and rest, especially toward the morning, the distribution being finished. Those that are very cold, and especially in their feet, cannot get to sleep; the cause may be that in sleep is required a free respiration, which cold doth shut in and hinder. Therefore, we have nothing else to advise but that men keep themselves hot in their sleep.

Sleep is regularly due unto human nature once within four-and-twenty hours, and that for six or five hours at the least; though there are, even in this kind, sometimes miracles of nature; as it is recorded of Mæcenas, that he slept not for a long time before his death. The fable tells us that Epimenides slept many years together in a cave, and all that time needed no meat; because the spirits waste not much in sleep.

Some noises help sleep; as the blowing of the wind, the trickling of water, humming of bees, soft singing, reading, etc. The cause is that they move in the spirits a gentle attention; and whatsoever moveth attention, without too much labor, stilleth the natural and discursive

[130]

motion of the spirits. Sleep nourisheth, or at least preserveth, bodies a long time, without other nourishment.

There have some been found who sustained themselves—almost to a miracle in nature—a very long time without meat or drink. Living creatures may subsist somewhat the longer without aliment, if they sleep; now, sleep is nothing else but a reception and retirement of the living spirit into itself. Experience teacheth us that certain creatures, as dormice and bats, sleep in some close places a whole winter together; such is the force of sleep to restrain all vital consumption. That which bees or drones are also thought to do, though sometimes destitute of honey; and likewise butterflies and other flies. Beasts that sleep in winter,—as it is noted of wild bears,—during their sleep wax very fat, though they eat nothing. Bats have been found in ovens, and other hollow close places, matted one upon another; and, therefore, it is likely that they sleep in the winter time, and eat nothing. Butterflies, and other flies, do not only sleep, but lie as dead all winter; and yet with a little heat of sun or fire, revive again. A dormouse, both winter and summer, will sleep some days together, and eat nothing.

Sleep after dinner—the stomach sending up no unpleasing vapors to the head, as being the first dews of our meat—is good for the spirits, but derogatory and hurtful to all other points of health. Notwithstanding, in extreme old age there is the same reason of meat and sleep; for both our meals and our sleeps should be then frequent, but short and little; nay, and toward the last period of old age, a mere rest, and, as it were, a perpetual reposing, doth best—especially in winter time.

To be free-minded and cheerfully disposed at hours of meat and of sleep and of exercise, is one of the best precepts of long lasting.

[131]

We suppose that a good clothing of the body maketh much to long life, for it fenceth and armeth against the intemperances of the air, which do wonderfully assail and decay the body.

Above all things, in youth, and for those that have sufficiently strong stomachs, it will be best to take a good draught of clear cold water when they go to bed.

Washing the body in cold water is good for length of life.

Especially, care must be taken that no hot things be applied to the head outwardly.

Not only the goodness or pureness of the air, but also the equality of the air, is material to long life. It is a secret that the healthfulness of air, especially in any perfection, is better found by experiment than by discourse or conjecture. The country life is well fitted for long life; it is much abroad, and in the open air; it is not slothful, but ever in employment. They are longer lived, for the most part, that live abroad in the open air, than they that live in houses; and it is certain that the morning air is more lively and refreshing than the evening air. Change of air by traveling, after one be used unto it, is good; and, therefore, great travelers have been long-lived. Also those that have lived perpetually in a little cottage, in the same place, have been long livers; for air accustomed consumeth less, but air changed nourisheth and repaireth more.

The heart receiveth benefit or harm most from the air which we breathe, from vapors, and from the affections.

We must come now to the affections and passions of the mind, and see which of them are hurtful to long life, which profitable.

Every noble, and resolute, and—as they call it—heroical desire, strengtheneth and enlargeth the powers of the heart. Goodness I call the habit, and goodness of nature the inclination. This, of all virtues and dignities of the mind, is the greatest, being the character of the Deity; and without it, man is a busy, mischievous, wretched thing, no better than a kind of vermin.

Hope is the most beneficial of all the affections, and doth much to the prolongation of life, if it be not too often frustrated, but entertaineth the fancy with an expectation of good, therefore, they which fix and propound to themselves some end,—as the mark and scope of their life,—and continually and by degrees go forward in the same, are, for the most part, long-lived.

Admiration and light contemplation are very powerful to the prolonging of life; for they hold the spirits in such things as delight them, and suffer them not to tumultuate, or to carry themselves unquietly and waywardly. Therefore, all the contemplators of natural things, which had so many and eminent objects to admire, were long-lived.

Action, endeavor, and labor, undertaken cheerfully and with a good will, doth refresh the spirits; but with an aversation and unwillingness, doth fret and deject them. Therefore it conferreth to long life, either that a man hath the art to institute his life so as it may be free and suitable to his own humor, or else to lay such a command upon his mind, that whatsoever is imposed by fortune, it may rather lead him than drag him.

No doubt it furthereth long life, to have all things from our youth to our elder age mend and grow to the better; that a youth full of crosses may minister sweetness to our old age.

One thing, above all, is grateful to the spirits: that there be a continual progress to the more benign. Therefore we should lead such a youth and manhood, that our old age should find new solaces, whereof the chief is moderate ease; and, therefore, old men in honorable places lay violent hands upon themselves, who retire not to their ease. But this thing doth require two cautions: one, that they drive not off till their bodies be utterly worn out and diseased, for in such bodies all mutation, though to the more benign, hasteneth death; the other, that they surrender not themselves to a sluggish ease, but that they embrace something which may entertain their thoughts and mind with contentation.

Ficino saith—not unwisely—that old men, for the comforting of their spirits, ought often to remember and ruminate upon the acts of their childhood and youth. Certainly, such a remembrance is a kind of peculiar recreation to every old man; and, therefore, it is a delight to men to enjoy the society of them which have been brought up together with them, and to visit the places of their education. Vespasian did attribute so much to this matter, that, when he was emperor, he would by no means be persuaded to leave his father's house,—though but mean,—lest he should lose the wonted object of his eyes and the memory of his childhood. And, besides, he would drink in a wooden cup tipped with silver, which was his grandmother's, upon festival days.

The spirits are delighted both with wonted things and with new. Now, it maketh wonderfully to the conservation of the spirits in vigor, that we neither use wonted things to a satiety and glutting, nor new things before a quick and strong appetite. Therefore, both customs are to be broken off with judgment and care, before they breed a fullness; and the appetite after new things to be restrained for a time, until it grow more sharp and jocund. Moreover, the life, as much as may be, is so to be ordered, that it may have many renovations; and the spirits, by perpetual conversing in the same actions, may not wax dull. For though it were no ill saying of Seneca's, "The fool doth ever begin to live"; yet this folly, and many more such, are good for long life.

It is to be observed touching the spirits,—though the contrary used to be done,—that when men perceive their spirits to be in good, placid, and healthful state,— that which will be seen by the tranquillity of their mind, and cheerful disposition,—that they cherish them, and not change them; but when in a turbulent and untoward state,—which will also appear by their sadness, lumpishness, and other indisposition of their mind,—that then they straight overwhelm them and alter them. Now, the spirits are contained in the same state by a restraining of the affections, temperateness of diet, moderation in labor, indifferent rest and respose, and the contrary to these do alter and overwhelm the spirits; as, namely, vehement affections, profuse feastings, difficult labors, earnest studies, and prosecution of business. Yet men are wont, when they are merriest and best disposed, then to apply themselves to feastings, labors, endeavors, business; whereas, if they have a regard to long life,—which may seem strange,—they should rather practice the contrary. For we ought to cherish and preserve good spirits; and for the evil-disposed spirits, to discharge and alter them.

Grief and sadness, if it be void of fear, and afflict not too much, doth rather prolong life.

Great joys attenuate and diffuse the spirits, and shorten life. Great fears, also, shorten life; for though grief and fear do both strengthen the spirits, yet in grief there is a simple contraction; but in fear, by reason of the cares taken for the remedy, and hopes intermixed, there is a turmoil and vexing of the spirits.

Whosoever is out of patience, is out of possession of his soul.

[135]

Envy is the worst of all passions, and feedeth upon the spirits, and they again upon the body. Of all affections, envy is the most importune and continual; therefore it was well said, "Envy keeps no holidays," for it is ever working upon some or other. It is also the vilest affection, and the most depraved; for which cause it is the proper attribute of the devil, who is called "The envious man, that soweth tares amongst the wheat by night."

Certainly, the more a man drinketh of the world, the more it intoxicateth. I cannot call riches better than the baggage of virtue. The Roman word is better, "impedimenta"; for as the baggage is to an army, so is riches to virtue; it cannot be spared nor left behind, but it hindereth the march; yea, and the care of it sometimes loseth or disturbeth the victory.

It is most certain, that passions always covet and desire that which experience forsakes. And they all know, who have paid dear for serving and obeying their lusts, that whether it be honor, or riches, or delight, or glory, or knowledge, or anything else, which they seek after; yet are they but things cast off, and, by divers men in all ages, after experience had, utterly rejected and loathed.

There is a wisdom in this beyond the rules of physic: a man's own observation, what he finds good of, and what he finds hurt of, is the best physic to preserve health. But it is a safer conclusion to say, "This agreeth not well with me, therefore I will not continue it"; than this, "I find no offense of this, therefore I may use it"; for strength of nature in youth passeth over many excesses which are owing a man till his age. Discern of the coming on of years, and think not to do the same things still; for age will not be defied. Beware of sudden change in any great point of diet, and, if necessity enforce it, fit the rest to it; for it is a secret both in nature and state, that it is safer to change many things than one. Examine thy customs of diet, sleep, exercise, apparel, and the like; and try, in anything thou shalt judge hurtful, to discontinue it by little and little.

Entertain hopes; mirth rather than joy; variety of delights, rather than surfeit of them; wonder and admiration, and therefore novelties; studies that fill the mind with splendid and illustrious objects, as histories, fables, and contemplations of nature. If you fly physic in health altogether, it will be too strange for your body when you shall need it; if you make it too familiar, it will work no extraordinary effect when sickness cometh. Despise no new accident in your body, but ask opinion of it. In sickness, respect health principally; and in health, action; for those that put their bodies to endure in health, may, in most sicknesses which are not very sharp, be cured only with diet and tendering.

Physicians are some of them so pleasing and conformable to the humor of the patient, as they press not the true cure of the disease; and some others are so regular in proceeding according to art for the disease, as they respect not sufficiently the condition of the patient. Take one of a middle temper; or, if it may not be found in one man, combine two of either sort; and forget not to call as well the best acquainted with your body, as the best reputed of for his faculty.

Touching the length and shortness of life in living creatures, the information which may be had is but slender, observation negligent, and tradition fabulous. In tame creatures, their degenerate life corrupteth them; in wild creatures, their exposing to all weathers often intercepteth them.

Man's age, as far as can be gathered by any certain narration, doth exceed the age of all other living

creatures, except it be of a very few only. No doubt
there are times in every country wherein men are longer
or shorter lived: longer, for the most part, when they
fare less deliciously, and are more given to bodily exercises; shorter, when they abandon themselves to luxury
and ease. The countries which have been observed to
produce long livers are these: Arcadia, Ætolia, India
on this side Ganges, Brazil, Taprobane [Ceylon], Britain,
Ireland, with the islands of the Orcades [Orkneys] and
Hebrides. We read that the Esseans [Essenes], amongst
the Jews, did usually extend their life to a hundred
years. Now, that sect used a single or abstemious diet,
after the rule of Pythagoras. The monks and hermits,
which fed sparingly, and upon dry aliment, attained
commonly to a great age. Amongst the Venetians there
have been found not a few long livers, and those of the
more eminent sort: Francis Donato, Duke; Thomas
Contarini, Procurator of St. Mark; and others. But
most memorable is Cornaro the Venetian; who, being
in his youth of a sickly body, began first to eat and drink
by measure to a certain weight, thereby to recover his
health; this cure turned by use into a diet; that diet to
an extraordinary long life, even of a hundred years and
better, without any decay in his senses, and with a constant enjoying of his health.

Being admonished by Aristotle's observation touching plants, that the putting forth of new shoots and
branches refresheth the body of the tree in the passage;
we conceive the like reason might be, if the flesh and
blood in the body of man were often renewed, that
thereby the bones themselves, and membranes, and other
parts,—which in their own nature are less reparable,—
partly by the cheerful passage of the juices, partly by
that new clothing of the young flesh and blood, might
be watered and renewed. If any man could procure

that a young man's spirit could be conveyed into an old man's body, it is not unlikely but this great wheel of the spirits might turn about the lesser wheels of the parts, and so the course of nature become retrograde. The spirit, if it be not irritated by the antipathy of the body inclosing it, nor fed by the overmuch likeness of that body, nor solicited nor invited by the external body, makes no great stir to get out.

We denounce unto men that they will give over trifling, and not imagine that so great a work as the stopping and turning back the powerful course of nature can be brought to pass by some morning draught, or the taking of some precious drug; but that they would be assured that it must needs be that this is a work of labor, and consisteth of many remedies, and a fit connection of them amongst themselves.

If a man perform that which hath not been attempted before, or attempted and given over, or hath been achieved, but not with so good circumstance, he shall purchase more honor than by affecting a matter of greater difficulty, or virtue, wherein he is but a follower.

Experience, no doubt, will both verify and promote these matters. And such, in all things, are the works of every prudent counsel, that they are admirable in their effects.

Voluptuous man
Is by superior faculties misled;
Misled from pleasure even in quest of joy,
Sated with Nature's boons, what thousands seek,
With dishes tortur'd from their native taste,
And mad variety, to spur beyond
Its wiser will the jaded appetite!
Is this for pleasure? Learn a juster taste!
And know that temperance is true luxury.

Know, whate'er
Beyond its natural fervor hurries on
The sanguine tide; whether the frequent bowl,
High-season'd fare, or exercise to toil
Protracted; spurs to its last stage tired life,
And sows the temples with untimely snow

—John Armstrong.

SELECTED AND ARRANGED FROM

SIR WILLIAM TEMPLE'S

"HEALTH AND LONG LIFE"

ETC.*

I can truly say, that, of all the paper I have blotted, which has been a great deal in my time, I have never written anything for the public without the intention of some public good. Whether I have succeeded, or no, is not my part to judge; and others, in what they tell me, may deceive either me or themselves. Good intentions are at least the seed of good actions; and every man ought to sow them, and leave it to the soil and the seasons whether they come up or no, and whether he or any other gathers the fruit.

I have chosen those subjects of these essays, wherein I take human life to be most concerned, and which are

* See Note C

of most common use, or most necessary knowledge; and wherein, though I may not be able to inform men more than they know, yet I may, perhaps, give them the occasion to consider more than they do. All men would be glad to be their own masters, and should not be sorry to be their own scholars, when they pay no more for their learning than their own thoughts, which they have commonly more store of about them than they know what to do with. Of all sorts of instructions, the best is gained from our own thoughts as well as experience; for though a man may grow learned by other men's thoughts, yet he will grow wise or happy only by his own—the use of other men's toward these ends, is but to serve for one's own reflections.

Some writers, in casting up the goods most desirable in life, have given them this rank: health, beauty, and riches. Of the first I find no dispute, but to the two others much may be said; for beauty is a good that makes others happy rather than one's self; and how riches should claim so high a rank, I cannot tell, when so great, so wise, and so good a part of mankind have, in all ages, preferred poverty before them. All the ancient philosophers—whatever else they differed in—agreed in this of despising riches, and at best esteeming them an unnecessary trouble or encumbrance of life; so that whether they are to be reckoned among goods or evils is yet left in doubt.

The two great blessings of life are, in my opinion, health and good humor; and none contribute more to one another. Without health, all will allow life to be but a burden; and the several conditions of fortune to be all wearisome, dull, or disagreeable, without good humor; nor does any seem to contribute toward the true happiness of life, but as it serves to increase that

[142]

treasure, or to preserve it. Whatever other differences are commonly apprehended in the several conditions of fortune, none, perhaps, will be found so true or so great as what is made by those two circumstances, so little regarded in the common course or pursuits of mortal men.

Health in the body is like peace in the State and serenity in the air. Health is the soul that animates all enjoyments of life, which fade and are tasteless, if not dead, without it. A man starves at the best and the greatest tables, and is poor and wretched in the midst of the greatest treasures and fortunes. With common diseases, strength grows decrepit; youth loses all vigor, and beauty all charms; music grows harsh, and conversation disagreeable; palaces are prisons, or of equal confinement; riches are useless; honor and attendance are cumbersome; and crowns themselves are a burden. But if diseases are painful and violent, they equal all conditions of life, and make no difference between a prince and a beggar The vigor of the mind decays with that of the body, and not only humor and invention, but even judgment and resolution, change and languish with ill constitution of body and of health; and, by this means, public business comes to suffer by private infirmities, and Kingdoms or States fall into weaknesses and distempers or decays of those persons that manage them. I have seen the counsels of a noble country grow bold or timorous, according to the fits of his good or ill health that managed them; and the pulse of the government beat high or low with that of the governor. Thus, accidents of health grow to be accidents of State; and public constitutions come to depend, in a great measure, upon those of particular men.

To know that the passions or distempers of the mind

[143]

make our lives unhappy, in spite of all accidents and favors of fortune, a man, perhaps, must be a philosopher and requires much thought, and study, and deep reflections. To be a Stoic, and grow insensible of pain, as well as poverty or disgrace, one must be, perhaps, something more or less than a man, renounce common nature, oppose common truth and constant experience. But there needs little learning or study, more than common thought and observation, to find out that ill health loses not only the enjoyments of fortune, but the pleasures of sense, and even of imagination; and hinders the common operations both of body and mind from being easy and free. Let philosophers reason and differ about the chief good or happiness of man; let them find it where they can, and place it where they please; but there is no mistake so gross, or opinion so impertinent,—how common soever,—as to think pleasures arise from what is without us, rather than from what is within.

But to leave philosophy, and return to health. Whatever is true in point of happiness depending upon the temper of the mind, 'tis certain that pleasures depend upon the temper of the body; and that, to enjoy them, a man must be well himself. Men are apt to play with their health and their lives, as they do with their clothes. To find any felicity, or take any pleasure in the greatest advantages of honor and fortune, a man must be in health. Who would not be covetous, and with reason, if this could be purchased with gold? who not ambitious, if it were at the command of power, or restored by honor? But, alas! a white staff will not help gouty feet to walk better than a common cane: nor a blue ribbon bind up a wound so well as a fillet; the glitter of gold or of diamonds will but hurt sore eyes, instead of curing them; and an aching head will be no more eased by wearing a crown than a common nightcap.

If health be such a blessing, and the very source of all pleasure, it may be worth the pains to discover the regions where it grows, the springs that feed it, the customs and methods by which it is best cultivated and preserved. Toward this end, it will be necessary to consider the examples or instances we meet with of health, and long life, which is the consequence of it; and to observe the places, the customs, and the conditions of those who enjoyed them in any degree extraordinary; from whence we may best guess at the causes, and make the truest conclusions.

Health and long life are usually blessings of the poor, not of the rich; and the fruits of temperance, rather than of luxury and excess. And, indeed, if a rich man does not, in many things, live like a poor, he will certainly be the worse for his riches: if he does not use exercise, which is but voluntary labor; if he does not restrain appetite by choice, as the other does by necessity; if he does not practice sometimes even abstinence and fasting, which is the last extreme of want and poverty. If his cares and his troubles increase with his riches, or his passions with his pleasures, he will certainly impair in health, whilst he improves his fortunes, and lose more than he gains by the bargain; since health is the best of all human possessions, and without which the rest are not relished or kindly enjoyed.

It is observable in story, that the ancient philosophers lived generally very long; which may be attributed to their great temperance, and their freedom from common passions, as well as cares, of the world. The Brazilians, when first discovered, lived the most natural original lives of mankind, so frequently described in ancient countries, before laws, or property, or arts made entrance among them; they lived without business or labor, further than for their necessary food, by gathering fruits, herbs, and plants; they knew no drink but water; were not tempted to eat nor drink beyond common thirst or appetite; were not troubled with either public or domestic cares; nor knew any pleasures but the most simple and natural. Many of these were said, at the time that country was discovered by the Europeans, to have lived two hundred, some three hundred years.

From these examples and customs it may probably be concluded, that the common ingredients of health and long life—where births are not impaired from the conception by any derived infirmities of the race they come from—are great temperance, open air, easy labor, little care, simplicity of diet, and water—which preserves the radical moisture without too much increasing the radical heat; whereas sickness, decay, and death proceed commonly from the one preying too fast upon the other, and at length wholly extinguishing it.

I think temperance deserves the first rank among public virtues, as well as those of private men; and doubt whether any can pretend to the constant, steady exercise of prudence, justice, or fortitude, without it. That which I call temperance, is a regular and simple diet, limited by every man's experience of his own easy digestion, and thereby proportioning, as near as well can be, the daily repairs to the daily decays of our wasting bodies. Temperance, that virtue without pride, and fortune without envy! that gives indolence [repose] of body, and tranquillity of mind; the best guardian of youth, and support of old age; the precept of reason, as well as religion; the physician of the soul, as well as the body; the tutelar goddess of health, and universal medicine of life; that clears the head, and cleanses the blood; that strengthens the nerves, enlightens the eyes, and comforts the heart!

No degree of temperance can, I think, be too great for the cure of most diseases to which mankind is exposed, rather by the viciousness, than by the frailty, of their natures—diseases by which we often condemn ourselves to greater torments and miseries of life than have, perhaps, been yet invented by anger or revenge, or inflicted by the greatest tyrants upon the worst of men. I know not whether some desperate degrees of abstinence would not have the same effect upon other men, as they had upon Atticus; who, weary of his life as well as his physicians by long and cruel pains of a dropsical gout, and despairing of any cure, resolved by degrees to starve himself to death; and went so far, that the physicians found he had ended his disease instead of his life.

For one life that ends by mere decay of nature or age, millions are intercepted by accidents from without or diseases within; by untimely deaths or decays; from the effects of excess and luxury, immoderate repletion or exercise. Men are, perhaps, most betrayed to all these dangers by great strength and vigor of constitution, by more appetite and larger fare, in colder climates; in the warm, excesses are found more pernicious to health, and so more avoided; and if experience and reflection do not cause temperance among them, yet it is forced upon them by the faintness of appetite. I can find no better account of a story Sir Francis Bacon tells, of a very old man, whose customs and diet he inquired; who said he observed none besides eating before he was hungry and drinking before he was dry, for by that rule he was sure never to eat nor drink much at a time. I do not remember, either in story or modern observa-

tion, any examples of long life common to any parts of
Europe, which the temper of the climate has probably
made the scene of luxury and excesses in diet.

And, I doubt, pleasures too long continued, or rather
too frequently repeated, may spend the spirits, and
thereby life, too fast, to leave it very long; like blowing
a fire too often, which makes it indeed burn the better,
but last the less. For as pleasures perish themselves
in the using,—like flowers that fade with gathering,—
so 'tis neither natural nor safe to continue them long,
to renew them without appetite, or ever to provoke
them by arts or imagination where Nature does not
call; who can best tell us when and how much we need,
or what is good for us, if we were so wise as to consult
her.

The faintness of appetite, especially in great cities,
makes the many endeavors to relieve and provoke it by
art, where nature fails; and this is one great ground of
luxury, and so many, and various, and extravagant
inventions to heighten and improve it; which may serve
perhaps for some refinement in pleasure, but not at all
for any advantages of health or of life. On the contrary, all the great cities, celebrated most by the concourse of mankind, and by the inventions and customs
of the greatest and most delicate luxury, are the scenes
of the most frequent and violent plagues, as well as
other diseases.

In the course of common life, a man must either
often exercise, or fast, or take physic, or be sick; and
the choice seems left to everyone as he likes. The first
two are the best methods and means of preserving
health; the use of physic is for restoring it, and curing
those diseases which are generally caused by the want
or neglect of the others; but is neither necessary, nor

[148]

perhaps useful, for confirming health, or to the length of life, being generally a force upon nature—though the end of it seems to be rather assisting nature, than opposing it in its course. Nature knows her own wants and times so well, as to need little assistance; leave her to her course, who is the sovereign physician in most diseases, and leaves little for others to do.

'Tis true, physicians must be in danger of losing their credit with the vulgar, if they should often tell a patient he has no need of physic, and prescribe only rules of diet or common use; most people would think they had lost their fee. But the first excellence of a physician's skill and care is discovered by resolving whether it be best in the case to administer any physic or none—to trust to nature or to art; and the next, to give such prescriptions, as, if they do no good, may be sure to do no harm.

In the midst of such uncertainties of health and of physic, for my own part, I have, in the general course of my life, trusted to God Almighty; to nature; to temperance or abstinence; and the use of common remedies, vulgarly known and approved, like proverbs, by long observation and experience, either of my own, or such persons as have fallen in the way of my observation or inquiry. The best cares or provisions for life and health consist in the discreet and temperate government of diet and exercise, in both which all excess is to be avoided.

As hope is the sovereign balsam of life, and the best cordial in all distempers both of body or mind; so fear, and regret, and melancholy apprehensions—with the distractions, disquiets, or at least intranquillity, they occasion—are the worst accidents that can attend any diseases; and make them often mortal, which would otherwise pass, and have had but a common course. I have known the most busy ministers of state, most fortunate courtiers, most vigorous youths, most beautiful virgins, in the strength or flower of their age, sink under common distempers, by the force of such weights, and the cruel damps and disturbances thereby given their spirits and their blood. 'Tis no matter what is made the occasion, if well improved by spleen and melancholy apprehensions: a disappointed hope, a blot of honor, a strain of conscience, an unfortunate love, an aching jealousy, a repining grief, will serve the turn, and all alike.

I remember an ingenious physician, who told me, in the fanatic times, he found most of his patients so disturbed by troubles of conscience, that he was forced to play the divine with them before he could begin the physician; whose greatest skill, perhaps, often lies in the infusing of hopes, and inducing some composure and tranquillity of mind, before he enters upon the other operations of his art. This ought to be the first endeavor of the patient, too; without which, all other medicines may lose their virtue. In all diseases of body or mind, it is happy to have an able physician for a friend, or discreet friend for a physician; which is so great a blessing, that the wise man will have it to proceed only from God, where he says: "A faithful friend is the medicine of life, and he that fears the Lord shall find him."

Greece, having been the first scene of luxury we meet with in story, and having thereby occasioned more diseases, seemed to owe the world that justice of providing the remedies. Among the more simple and original customs and lives of other nations it entered late, and was introduced by the Grecians. In ancient Baby-

SIR WILLIAM TEMPLE
1628—1699

From the painting by Sir Peter Lely—No. 152, National Portrait Gallery,
London

Photograph copyrighted by Walker and Cockerell

lon—how great and populous soever—no physicians were known, nor other methods for the cure of diseases, besides abstinence, patience, and domestic care.

Whoever was accounted the god of physic, the prince of this science must be by all, I think, allowed to have been Hippocrates, whose writings are the most ancient of any that remain to posterity. He was a great philosopher and naturalist, before he began the study of physic, to which both these are perhaps necessary. His rules and methods continued in practice as well as esteem, without any dispute, for many ages, till the time of Galen; and I have heard a great physician say, that his aphorisms are still the most certain and uncontrolled of any that science has produced. I will judge but of one, which, in my opinion, has the greatest race and height both of sense and judgment that I have read in so few words, and the best expressed: "Ars longa, vita brevis, experientia fallax, occasio præceps, judicium difficile" ["Art is long, life is short, experience deceptive, opportunity sudden, decision difficult"]. By which alone, if no more remained of that admirable person, we may easily judge how great a genius he was, and how perfectly he understood both nature and art. In the time of Adrian, Galen began to change the practice and methods of physic, derived to that age from Hippocrates; and those of his new institution continue generally observed to our time. Yet Paracelsus, about two hundred years ago, endeavored to overthrow the whole scheme of Galen, and introduce a new one of his own, as well as the use of chemical medicines; and has not wanted his followers and admirers ever since.

I have, in my life, met with two of above a hundred and twelve; whereof the woman had passed her life in service; and the man, in common labor, till he grew old, and fell upon the parish. But I met with one who had gone a much greater length, which made me more curious in my inquiries: 'twas an old man, who told me he was a hundred and twenty-four years old. I have heard, and very credibly, of many in my life, above a hundred years old.

One comfort of age may be, that, whereas younger men are usually in pain, when they are not in pleasure, old men find a sort of pleasure, whenever they are out of pain. And, as young men often lose or impair their present enjoyments, by raving after what is to come, by vain hopes, or fruitless fears; so old men relieve the wants of their age, by pleasing reflections upon what is past. Therefore men, in the health and vigor of their age, should endeavor to fill their lives with the worthiest actions,—either in their public or private stations,—that they may have something agreeable left to feed on, when they are old, by pleasing remembrances. But, as they are only the clean beasts which chew the cud, when they have fed enough; so they must be clean and virtuous men that can reflect, with pleasure, upon the past accidents or courses of their lives. Besides, men who grow old with good sense, or good fortunes, and good nature, cannot want the pleasure of pleasing others, by assisting with their gifts, their credit, and their advice, such as deserve it.

Socrates used to say, that 'twas pleasant to grow old with good health and a good friend. But there cannot indeed live a more unhappy creature than an ill-natured old man, who is neither capable of receiving pleasures, nor sensible of doing them to others; and, in such a condition, it is time to leave them.

Thus have I traced, in this essay, whatever has fallen

in my way or thoughts to observe concerning life and health, and which I conceived might be of any public use to be known or considered; the plainness wherewith it is written easily shows there could be no other intention; and it may at least pass, like a Derbyshire charm, which is used among sick cattle, with these words: "If it does thee no good, it will do thee no harm."

I would recommend to everyone that admirable precept which Pythagoras is said to have given to his disciples . . . . "Pitch upon that course of life which is the most excellent, and custom will render it the most delightful." Men whose circumstances will permit them to choose their own way of life are inexcusable if they do not pursue that which their judgment tells them is the most laudable. The voice of reason is more to be regarded than the bent of any present inclination, since, by the rule above mentioned, inclination will at length come over to reason, though we can never force reason to comply with inclination.—Joseph Addison.

APPENDIX

A Short History
of
The Cornaro Family

Some Account
of
Eminent Cornaros

A Eulogy upon Louis Cornaro
by
Bartolomeo Gamba

"The Villas Erected by Louis Cornaro"
by
Dr. Prof. Emilio Lovarini

Health, brightest visitant from heaven,
   Grant me with thee to rest!
For the short term by nature given,
   Be thou my constant guest!
For all the pride that wealth bestows,
The pleasure that from children flows,
Whate'er we court in regal state
That makes men covet to be great,

Whatever sweets we hope to find
   In Love's delightful snare;
Whatever good by Heaven assign'd,
   Whatever pause from care:
All flourish at thy smile divine,
The spring of loveliness is thine,
And every joy that warms our hearts,
With thee approaches and departs.

                          —Robert Bland.

A SHORT HISTORY

OF

THE ANCIENT AND ILLUSTRIOUS

CORNARO FAMILY

OF VENICE

Nor can the skillful herald trace
The founder of thy ancient race.
                              —Jonathan Swift.

The noble steeds, and harness bright,
And gallant lord, and stalwart knight,
In rich array—
Where shall we seek them now? Alas!
Like the bright dewdrops on the grass,
They passed away.
                    —Manrique (trans. by Longfellow).

NEVER was parent better repaid by the steadfast devo-
tion of her children than was that Mistress of the
Seas, who, century after century, was the wonder
and admiration of mankind; the center of the trade and finance
of the world, supreme as she was in every mart; the most

[159]

valiant defender of civilization in its wars against the Turks; as well as the example to humanity, and its inspiration, in all the arts of peace.

Among her patriotic sons and daughters, none labored in her service with a more earnest self-denial than did the members of the illustrious patrician family of CORNARO, whose name is found interwoven for centuries in every honorable particular of the remarkable history of the Republic of Venice. Almost every line of the annals of this celebrated family shows unmistakably that their ambition, their aspiration, their toil, their courageous exposure—and often sacrifice—of life and fortune, were always for the advancement of their country's safety and glory, for which their own was counted as naught, determined, as they were, that Venice should excel in virtue, power, and splendor, any land which presumed to be her rival, and that her children should thus enjoy a life of happiness and security. This, for generations, was the ruling passion and guiding principle of this proud and noble family

The Cornari, the history of whom, for generations, added imperishable fame to their illustrious source, were descended, according to the most authoritative traditions of the chroniclers, from the ancient and noble race of the Cornelii* of Rome. Having in remote times settled at Rimini, they were subsequently among the first inhabitants of Rialto, the name by which Venice was known in its infancy. The orthography of the name, during the family's long history, was gradually modified, so that, from Cornelii, it became successively Cornelli, Coronelli, Coronetti, Coronarii, and finally Cornaro, or Corner. The names Corner and Cornaro are identical, the first being the abridged Italian form of the Venetian Cornaro; in the 18th century some members of the family adopted that of Corner, by which all are now known. (To be uniform, the ancient mode, that of Cornaro, is adhered to throughout this work)

Having been enrolled among those who comprised the

* See Note L

body of the Venetian nobility, the Cornaros were included among the first twelve patrician families of the Republic, called the apostolical, or tribunal families, which for centuries gave the military tribunes to the Republic, many of the family were members also of the famous Great Council, established in 1172.

In the 14th century, the family separated into two distinct branches, the first of which was distinguished by contemporaries, and later by historians, by the name of Cornaro of the Great House; the other was that of Cornaro Piscopia, so called from the castle and fief of Piscopia which they had acquired in the island of Cyprus, and which, formerly the property of Giovanni Ibelini, Count of Jaffa, had come into the possession of this branch of the family by a grant from the king, in 1363, to Federico (Frederick) Cornaro. This was the branch to which Caterina (Catherine) Cornaro, Queen of Cyprus; Elena Lucrezia (Helen Lucretia) Cornaro, the famous scholar, and Louis Cornaro, the author of "The Temperate Life," belonged. After the ascent of Caterina to regal power, by her marriage, in 1468, to James of Lusignan, King of Cyprus, the branch known as Cornaro of the Great House was also designated by the name of Cornaro of the Queen. It was then, also, that the family quartered with their own the royal arms of Cyprus, as shown in their coat of arms on page six.

To attempt even a short biography of all the many distinguished members of this noted family would be impossible in a work of this nature, however, abbreviated sketches of the lives of a few among those most celebrated may be of interest to the reader, and are to be found elsewhere in this volume. Few family records, in any country, show so large a number of members who have, by such a variety of paths, attained exalted station. The list comprises a queen, four princely doges of the Venetian Republic, twenty-two procurators of St. Mark, nine cardinals, and a host of names made illustrious by noteworthy achievement. As valiant leaders in peace or war, as honored councillors and trusted diplomats; as reverend senators and magistrates, in letters, philosophy; the sciences, and the arts,—the descendants of the Cornelii have proudly blazoned a record upon the scroll of fame that few historic families can equal

Yet, of all this illustrious number, to that plain and unassuming gentleman and true nobleman, Louis Cornaro, the veteran author of "The Temperate Life," is due the greatest distinction—the gratitude of all mankind.

That the memory of the race of Cornaro is indelibly preserved in marble and granite, the palaces, once the homes of illustrious members of the family, many of the churches of Venice, built by their aid, and often wholly or in part at their expense; and the monuments, erected by reverent descendants or by a grateful country to do honor to the memory of individuals of this family,—emphatically though silently testify.

In the Church of Sant' Apostoli—built largely at the expense of the family, and rebuilt in 1750—is a magnificent Cornaro Chapel, supported by fanciful Corinthian pillars. This chapel—erected in 1575—contains the sepulchral urn of Marco (Mark) Cornaro, father of Queen Caterina, and that of her brother, the famous nobleman Giorgio (George) Cornaro—the husband of Elisabetta Morosini—who died July 31, 1527.

In the magnificent Italian-Gothic Church of Santi Giovanni e Paolo, better known as San Zanipolo, and often called The Westminster Abbey of Venice,—begun in 1234, but not finished until 1430,—is the gorgeous mausoleum of the Doge Marco Cornaro, the sarcophagus decorated with roses, the canopy above it adorned with five very beautiful statues, the work of the most celebrated Venetian sculptors of the Middle Ages; here also may be seen the sepulchral urn of Pietro (Peter) Cornaro, who died in 1361.

In the Church of San Salvatore,—begun in 1506 and completed about 1534,—where lie the remains of Queen Caterina, in the center of a Corinthian portico there is a beautiful monument erected to her memory in the year 1570, the relief representing her resigning her crown to Doge Agostino Barbarigo (the 74th doge of Venice, 1486-1501) ; as well as one erected in the 16th century to three Cornaro cardinals, Marco, Francesco (Francis), and Andrea (Andrew).

In the Church of Santa Maria Gloriosa dei Frari—designed about 1250, and containing the colossal monument of Titian, unveiled in 1853—is the chapel of Angelo Cornaro, sculptured in marble (15th century). In the Church of Santa Maria della Salute—founded in 1631 as a monument of thanksgiving for the cessation of the great plague, and thus known as one of The Great Plague Churches of Venice—is the sepulchral urn of Antonio (Anthony) Cornaro, rich in carvings (16th century) In the Church of San Pietro di Castello —the Cathedral of Venice from the earliest days of the Republic until 1807—is the urn of Filippo (Philip) Cornaro, very rich in ornaments (16th century). In the Seminary (Il Seminario) is the urn of another Antonio Cornaro, with bas-reliefs representing infants and griffins (16th century) There is also a Cornaro monument in the Church of I Tolentini

It is impossible to do justice, in this work, to the beauty and grandeur, or to the historic associations, of the several magnificent palaces in Venice, once the homes of members of the Cornaro family, but now either inhabited by strangers, or else converted to the use of the public or of the government; consequently, we shall allude to them very briefly.

At that part of the venerable city known as Sant' Apostoli, is a Cornaro Palace of the 16th century, the whole façade of which was originally painted in fresco. At San Samuele, and facing upon the Grand Canal, is an imposing Cornaro Palace, which, in the early part of the 18th century, was the home of the nobleman Girolamo (Jerome) Cornaro. Another, at San Canciano, was, in the 18th century, the home of the senator and famous author Flaminio (Flaminius) Cornaro.

At San Cassiano, in the Street of the Queen, is the Cor-

naro Palace of the Queen, the old name of palace and street
being still retained; here was born, in 1454, Caterina Cornaro,
afterward Queen of Cyprus. The ancient pile, however, does
not exist, the present one having been erected upon the site
of the old one in 1724 The new edifice, inelegant in style,
manifests the decadence of art, but the entrance from the
Grand Canal is really imposing, and is said to have cost an
immense sum. This structure is now a Mount of Piety
(Italian, Monte di pietà), a government establishment, the
object of which is to lend money, no matter how small in
amount, at only a nominal interest, to those who are in necessity; this custom, originating in Italy in the 15th century,
has since been adopted in various countries

Giovanni (John) Cornaro, nephew of Queen Caterina,
built, in 1548, upon an old site in the square of San Polo, what
is now known as the great Cornaro-Mocenigo-Revedin Palace,
of which Sammicheli was the architect. This palace gave to
the neighboring street the name of Cornaro. The Cornaro
Palace of the Great House, a massive and magnificent pile,
with a Doric, Ionic, and Composite front, was erected (by
Sansovino) in 1532, at San Maurizio, by the nephews of Queen
Caterina; it faces the Grand Canal, and is now the office of
the Royal Prefect of the Province There are two other Cor-
naro Palaces on the Grand Canal: one in the Court of the
Tree, now called the Cornaro-Spinelli Palace, a work of the
Renaissance; the other, at San Benedetto, at the corner of the
Canal of the Mails, is now called the Cornaro-Mocenigo
Palace, and is used as the office of the city's water-works.

The Cornaro-Piscopia Palace at San Luca—later called,
and still known as, the Loredan Palace, and now used as the
palace (or offices) of the municipality of Venice—was, in the
14th century, the residence of Federico Cornaro, whose guest
Peter of Lusignan, King of Cyprus, was in 1363 and 1364.
To show his gratitude, in addition to the grant of the fief of
Piscopia in his kingdom, the King created Cornaro a knight
of an ancient Cyprian order, having for its motto "To maintain loyalty" ("Pour loyauté maintenir"). To perpetuate
the memory of this visit of the King, Cornaro caused to be

graven upon the front of his palace on the Grand Canal, the royal arms of Cyprus beside those of the Cornaros, together with the knightly emblem of his order, there they may be seen to this day. The exact age and origin of this palace, an early Byzantine one, are not known, but it is believed to date back as early as the 10th or 11th century. In "The Stones of Venice" Ruskin says of it: "Though not conspicuous and often passed with neglect, the Loredan Palace, will, I believe, be felt at last, by all who examine it carefully, to be the most beautiful of all the palaces in the whole extent of the Grand Canal It has been restored often, once in the Gothic, once in the Renaissance times—some writers say even rebuilt; but, if so, rebuilt in its old form" It was in this palace, in the year 1646, that that marvel of her age, Elena Lucrezia Cornaro, was born.

When the great name of Cornaro and the prosperity of the family were at their zenith, their sumptuous palaces were filled with memorials of the glorious history of their ancestors. These mute testimonials to the prowess of warriors, as well as to the victors in more peaceful pursuits, were to be seen in an abundance more than sufficient to satisfy the most ambitious.

Nor will the visitor in Venice, once familiar with its streets, have any reason for ignorance of the existence of the name of Cornaro, for here, too, will he be confronted by mementos of this ancient family.

At San Maurizio, the footway and bridge known as Cornaro Zaguri lead to the Cornaro Palace of the Great House, as the Street of the Queen, at San Cassiano, leads to the Cornaro Palace of the Queen; and the street which gives access to the Cornaro Palace that faces on the Grand Canal, at San Samuele, is still called Cornaro. Another, bearing the family name, is Cornaro Street, near the square of San Polo, named after the palace in the square

The Cornaro family began to be interested in the Paduan country for the first time, so far as is known by the records, in the year 1406, when Francesco Cornaro became the proprietor of a portion of the confiscated property of the ancient lords of Carrara—from 1318 to 1405 the sovereign lords of Padua The palace on the Via Melchiorre Cesarotti in Padua, built by Louis Cornaro, is still in existence, and is known as the Cornaro Palace.   In the Church of San Antonio in Padua, one of the most remarkable buildings in Italy,—begun about 1230 and completed in 1307,—there is a monument dedicated to Caterino Cornaro, General of the Republic of Venice in the wars against the Turks.

When Caterina became Queen of Cyprus, the power of the Cornaro family in that kingdom was naturally increased   It is certain, however, that they were not only residents of the island, but possessed considerable influence there, for a long time prior to this event; and it is known that, in the middle of the 14th century, their wealth and position were such that the king resorted to them for a considerable loan of money.   At the court of Cyprus, Venice was regularly represented by a consul, and some contemporaneous documents go to prove the zeal which the Venetian Senate showed in having his appointed salary paid, and in seeing, at the same time, that the debts contracted by that court with Venetian merchants and bankers should be discharged.   In one of these documents, dated September 17, 1455, it is deplored that "injustice should have been committed, to the damage of the heirs and claimants of Giovanni Cornaro", and, furthermore, that "the noble citizen Marco Cornaro," father of Caterina, "should have been injured in his rights in not receiving that which the king owed him " The tutelage of Venice over Cyprus was, indeed, so diligent as to interest the king in the solution of a question of water necessary for the good culture of the sugar-cane in the fief of the Cornaros.

But with the glory, the power, and the commanding influence of The Queen of the Adriatic, that, too, of the race of the Cornari has well-nigh departed.   The fortunes

and personality of a house whose opulence and greatness were seldom, if ever, surpassed by any of their countrymen, and the lives of whose sons and daughters have furnished themes for an almost endless number of writers, are
now but a memory. In Venice there are, to-day, five families
who bear the name, and who, as descendants of the old race,
are recognized as belonging to the Venetian patriciate. Not
a Cornaro, however, lives in the halls of his ancestors But
the patriotic fire of the lords of generations ago still burns
in the breasts of their children, proud of the history of their
family, they still hold Queen Caterina especially dear; and,
in order to perpetuate the memory of that noble woman, a
custom was long since instituted to give the name of Caterino
to a male child, in the event of the denial, to any family, of
a girl baby

Among the many portraits of the members of this celebrated family—not elsewhere mentioned in this work—is that
of Giorgio Cornaro, in the collection of the Earl of Carlisle;
and The Cornaro Family, in Alnwick Castle, the baronial
residence of the dukes of Northumberland,—both by Titian.

Man's rich with little, were his judgment true,
Nature is frugal, and her wants are few;
These few wants, answer'd, bring sincere delights;
But fools create themselves new appetites.

At thirty, man suspects himself a fool,
Knows it at forty, and reforms his plan;
At fifty, chides his infamous delay,
Pushes his prudent purpose to resolve,
In all the magnanimity of thought,
Resolves, and re-resolves, then dies the same.
And why?   Because he thinks himself immortal.
All men think all men mortal but themselves

—Edward Young.

SOME ACCOUNT

OF

EMINENT MEMBERS

OF

The Cornaro Family

PILGRIM,

FROM LIVES THUS SPENT THY EARTHLY DUTIES LEARN;
FROM FANCY'S DREAMS TO ACTIVE VIRTUE TURN:
LET FREEDOM, FRIENDSHIP, FAITH, THY SOUL ENGAGE,
AND SERVE, LIKE THEM, THY COUNTRY AND THY AGE.*

CATERINA (CATHERINE) CORNARO, one of the most illustrious women of the Renaissance, was the daughter of Marco Cornaro—grandson of the Doge Marco Cornaro—and Fiorenza, his wife; and was born in the city of Venice, November 25, 1454, in that Cornaro Palace to which—as well as to the present one, built in the 18th century on the site of the ancient structure—the fact of her birth

* From a mural tablet in The First Church, Quincy, Massachusetts, placed there in memory of John Adams, the second President of the United States, and Abigail Smith, his wife.

[169]

and of her subsequent elevation to royal power gave the name
of the Cornaro Palace of the Queen, and, to the street in which
it is located, the name of the Street of the Queen

Her brilliant, though mournful, history has afforded a
theme for many writers in all languages. Giving evidence
at an early age of rare qualities of mind, character, and person,—for there were few, if any, of her countrywomen who
excelled her in charm and grace,—she was educated with the
scrupulous care due the daughter of a royal house, as on her
mother's side she had an imperial ancestry by reason of her
descent from the Comneni emperors of Trebizond. She was
married July 10, 1468,—when not yet fifteen years of age,—
with the most gorgeous and extraordinary ceremonies and public rejoicings, to James of Lusignan, King of Cyprus, whose
love for her was first aroused on seeing her portrait in the
hands of her uncle, Andrea Cornaro; at the same time she was
adopted by the Venetian Senate as The Daughter of the
Republic, in order that her rank might equal that of her husband; and a dowry of one hundred thousand golden ducats
was presented to her

In 1473, on the death of her husband in his thirty-third
year, she succeeded him on the throne as Queen of Cyprus;
in August, 1474, she suffered the loss of the infant Prince
James, her only child—born August, 1473; and after a
troubled reign of sixteen years,—during which time she
acquired the well-deserved reputation of a very superior,
wise, energetic, liberal woman,—worried by political jealousies
and intrigues, she abdicated, February 26, 1489, in favor of
the Venetian Republic. On her return to Venice, she was
received with great pomp and consideration, the reigning
doge himself meeting her in the celebrated historic Bucentaur.* The beautiful country-seat and castle of Asolo, nine-
teen miles from Treviso and still in existence, was given her
in sovereignty, this, together with her palace in Venice, she
made her home for the remainder of her life, spending her
time in works of charity, in the cultivation of her rural
retreat, and in the pleasures of art and literature—maintain-
ing at Asolo a court for poets, scholars, and artists.

* See Note M

[170]

Her death occurred at Venice, July 10, 1510, and the body of the dead Queen was followed by all the dignitaries of Church and State, as well as by a vast concourse of citizens, to its resting-place in the Cornaro Chapel in the Church of Sant' Apostoli, whence it was removed in 1660, and placed in her mausoleum in the right transept of the Church of San Salvatore, where it now lies. The inscription, in Latin, plainly marks the final home of the remains of "Catherine, Queen of Cyprus, Jerusalem, and Armenia"

Her eminent relative, Cardinal Bembo, in his "Gli Asolani," pays a high tribute to her intellectual qualities, as well as her many womanly virtues. Her portrait, taken at the age of eighteen, in her crown and queenly robes, was painted by Titian; another, by Veronese, hangs in the Belvedere at Vienna; while the one by Pordenone is in the Dresden Gallery. A magnificent painting of her by Makart hangs in the National Gallery at Berlin; in it, as Queen of Cyprus, she is seen receiving the proffered homage of the Venetian patricians.

ELENA LUCREZIA (HELEN LUCRETIA) CORNARO PISCOPIA, one of the most accomplished and illustrious women of her day, was born at Venice, June 5, 1646, in the Cornaro Piscopia Palace—now the Loredan. She was the daughter of Giovanni Battista (John Baptist) Cornaro, Procurator of St Mark, and of Zanetta Boni, his wife.

Naturally of a very retiring as well as devotional disposition, she wished to enter some religious order, but her father's entreaties altered her purpose. For, recognizing, while she was still a child, her extraordinary gifts, he determined that nothing should interfere with his cherished ambition that his family should possess, in the person of his beautiful daughter,—though so delicate and modest, and averse to the world or to any kind of publicity,—the most learned woman of her day. This purpose he realized, albeit at the early sacrifice of the health, and, indeed, of the life, of the innocent victim of his paternal and ancestral pride.

[171]

Although entirely devoid of wordly ambition, yet, in order that she might not disappoint the parent whose every hope was centered in his daughter's triumph, she devoted all her energies to the task assigned her; so that, such were her wonderful powers of mind and memory, she soon excelled in every branch of learning. She acquired a perfect knowledge of many of the modern languages,—writing them with ease and speaking them fluently,—as well as of Latin, Greek, Hebrew, and Arabic. Her natural taste for poetry and music was so highly cultivated, that she sang, in a sweet and flexible voice, her own verses in various languages, set to music of her own composition, and to her own accompaniment, either on the viol, harp, or harpsichord. She became a perfect mistress of many of the arts and sciences, and of ancient and modern history, including, of course, that of her own country and family. In theology, philosophy, and dialectics she was no less accomplished In a word, her response to her father's appeal was so sincere that, although deaf to the applause of all,—nay, embarrassed by the admiration she constantly excited, distasteful to her as it was unavoidable,—she became a miracle of learning.

On a certain occasion, the haughty Venetian Senate went so far as to suspend an important session, in order that they might go in a body to hear a disputation in which, with that eloquence for which she was noted, she was engaged in the presence of an illustrious gathering, as was the fashion of the time. Contrary to her wishes, she was created a master of arts and doctor of philosophy by the renowned University of Padua,—founded early in the 13th century by the Emperor Frederick II,—receiving the title of Unalterable. The ceremony, which took place June 25, 1678, in the Cathedral of Padua, was attended by illustrious scholars of all countries, and was witnessed by an immense multitude, attracted by the unwonted spectacle. She was also elected to membership in all the principal literary societies of Italy At Rome, she was admitted at the University, and was entitled The Humble; and princes and representatives of all nations paid homage to her learning and virtues. Her hand was asked in marriage by some of the most noted men of her time; all of these offers, however, in obedience to a resolution made in her girlhood, she declined.

Her uninterrupted application to her studies, but especially the atmosphere of unwelcome publicity in which she had always lived,—so uncongenial and often painful to her sensitive nature,—completed the ruin of her naturally delicate health. Although anticipating her death to be not far distant, yet, to further please her father,—blind to her critical condition,—she wrote eulogies upon many of the most eminent personages of her day, these were followed by her remarkable panegyric on the Republic of Venice.

But the replies to these final efforts, which had been accomplished at such a fearful cost to her health and life, found the illustrious maiden stretched upon a bed of pain, which, in a short time, proved to be her couch of death—the release from her sufferings coming to her in the city of Padua, July 26, 1684. From that day to the 29th,—the day of her funeral,—when her body was laid to rest in the Church of Santa Giustina, the city, with all affairs suspended, presented the spectacle of a universal, heartfelt grief, so deeply in the affections of all was she enshrined Her death was recorded by poetical effusions from the learned of Europe. In an eloquent oration, pronounced at a funeral solemnity performed in her honor at Rome, she was celebrated as triumphing over three monsters, Pride, Luxury, and Ignorance At the foot of the staircase on the right of the entrance to the University of Padua, is a statue erected to her memory in 1773.

The first edition of her works was published at Parma in 1688

MARCO (MARK) CORNARO, the 59th doge of Venice, held that princely and historic office from July 21, 1365, to January 13, 1368, when he died at the age of eighty-two—one of the most famous doges of The Golden Book * During his term the Venetians waged a bitter war against the

* See Note N

Turks and, also, subdued the rebellion in Candia. His tomb is in the Church of Santi Giovanni e Paolo.

GIOVANNI (JOHN)—I.—CORNARO, the 96th doge of Venice, was elected January 4, 1625, as the successor of Francesco Contarini (doge, 1623-1624). During his reign the Venetians defended Mantua against the Imperial army, about which period a severe plague raged in Venice and throughout northern Italy. At this time, also, occurred a bitter feud between the powerful Zeno family—descendants of Renier Zeno, the 45th doge of Venice, 1253-1268—and his own. Cornaro died December 23, 1629.

FRANCESCO (FRANCIS) CORNARO, the 101st doge of Venice, was born May 6, 1585 He was the son of Doge Giovanni (I) Cornaro, and was chosen to his exalted office May 17, 1656. During his very short term—he died June 5 of the same year—the Venetians continued their victories over the Turks

GIOVANNI (JOHN)—II —CORNARO, the 111th doge of Venice, was born August 4, 1647. His mother, Cornelia Contarini, was of that illustrious family which gave the great Republic eight of its one hundred and twenty doges, a greater number than can be claimed for any other family. He was elected doge May 22, 1709 During his administration the Turks made war on Venice and, in 1715, took the Morea. He concluded these hostilities by the peace of Passarowitz, July 21, 1718. It was during his term that Venice lost her last possessions in the island of Candia. He died August 21, 1722. He married his relative, Laura Cornaro, who survived him, dying in May, 1729. He also left three sons, Francesco, Nicolò (Nicholas), and Alvise.

FEDERICO (FREDERICK) CORNARO, one of the three Venetian commanders in the struggle with the Genoese known as the War of Chioggia (1379-1381), impoverished himself by the voluntary sacrifice of his princely fortune to the use of his country. In August, 1379, when it was thought the Genoese might attack the city, arms were distributed to the people, and Cornaro was placed in command.

GIORGIO (GEORGE) CORNARO, nephew of the Doge Marco Cornaro, held during his lifetime many positions of trust and responsibility, both civil and military. He was a nobleman of sterling worth and considerable influence, his exalted patriotism inspiring ceaseless efforts for the welfare of his country; and such was the exposure consequent to his zeal in his profession of arms, that it caused the sacrifice of his health, and finally of his life, in her service. He died December, 1439, and his remains were followed by the entire population of Venice to their final resting-place in the Cornaro Chapel in the Church of Sant' Apostoli

ANDREA (ANDREW) CORNARO, a Venetian nobleman, and uncle of Caterina, Queen of Cyprus, was an extensive trader in that island He and his nephew, Marco Bembo, were murdered during the political disturbances subsequent to the death of Caterina's husband, King James

MARCO CORNARO, son of Giorgio Cornaro and Elisabetta Morosini his wife, and nephew of Queen Caterina, became Patriarch of Constantinople. He was a very eminent man and of great service to Venice. He died at that city, July 20, 1524.

FRANCESCO CORNARO was born in 1488. In early years he followed a military life, and became distinguished as a leader in the army of Venice in the wars—in which his country became involved—caused by the rival ambitions of Francis I., King of France, and Charles V., Emperor of Germany. When peace was secured he abandoned the profession of arms and devoted himself to politics and literature, becoming the ambassador of the Republic to the court of Charles V. He was a man of great learning, and, in 1527, was created a cardinal. He died September, 1543, in his fifty-fifth year, and was buried in the Church of San Salvatore, where his monument may still be seen.

ALVISE (LOUIS) CORNARO, Knight of Malta and Grand Prior of Cyprus, was born February 12, 1516, and died at Rome, May 10, 1584

FEDERICO CORNARO, son of the Doge Giovanni (I) Cornaro, was made Patriarch of Venice in 1632. He was Grand Prior of Cyprus, and died June 5, 1653, at the age of seventy-eight

GIROLAMO (JEROME) CORNARO was born June 25, 1632, he succeeded the illustrious Francesco Morosini as Captain-General of the Venetian army when, in 1688, the latter was elected the 108th doge of the Republic— the last of that family to attain the ducal dignity. Cornaro's valuable services to his country were, however, cut short in 1690 by his untimely death from fever at Valona,—a seaport town in Albania, European Turkey,—which the Turks had held since 1464, and the Venetians, under his command, had besieged and recovered His loss was regarded as a great calamity.

GIORGIO BASILIO (GEORGE BASIL) CORNARO, a younger brother of the Doge Giovanni (II) Cornaro, was born August 1, 1658. His early years were spent in the military service of his country; abandoning this, he entered the field of politics, holding many offices of considerable responsibility, for which his great learning, and the experience gained by extensive foreign travel, eminently qualified him In 1692 he represented Venice at the court of Portugal, and was later tendered the office of ambassador to the French king; this honor, however, he declined, preferring to embrace an ecclesiastical life He was a member of the order of

Knights of Malta, a religious and military order instituted in the 11th century; was also Grand Prior of Cyprus, an office hereditary in his family; and was made a cardinal July 22, 1697. He died August 10, 1722.

FLAMINIO (FLAMINIUS) CORNARO was born at Venice, February 4, 1693, where he died December 28, 1778. He was a Venetian Senator, and was distinguished for great learning, attaining eminence as a hagiographer, historian, and antiquarian. He was the author, in 1749, of a valuable work on the churches of Venice (15 vols.), and of another on those of Torcello (3 vols.) His home was the Cornaro Palace at San Canciano, in Venice.

ANDREA CORNARO was Governor of the island of Candia, and fell while fighting valiantly at Retimo, on the northern coast of the island.

Health is, indeed, so necessary to all the duties as well as pleasures of life, that the crime of squandering it is equal to the folly, and he that for a short gratification brings weakness and diseases upon himself, and for the pleasure of a few years passed in the tumults of diversion and clamors of merriment condemns the maturer and more experienced part of his life to the chamber and the couch, may be justly reproached, not only as a spendthrift of his happiness, but as a robber of the public; as a wretch that has voluntarily disqualified himself for the business of his station, and refused that part which Providence assigns him in the general task of human nature.—Samuel Johnson.

A EULOGY

UPON

Louis Cornaro

BY

BARTOLOMEO GAMBA *

DELIVERED ON THE TENTH DAY OF AUGUST, 1817, IN THE
ROYAL ACADEMY OF FINE ARTS OF VENICE, ON
THE OCCASION OF THE ANNUAL
DISTRIBUTION OF
PRIZES

ON this most impressive occasion, amid these appropriate surroundings, after the dignified speeches you have heard, I shrink from addressing you, my Lord Count the Governor, supreme magistrates of this city, most learned professors, worthy scholars—all of you, my kind hearers; but I speak in grateful submission to the honorable charge laid upon me, in obedience to the statutes of this Royal Academy, which direct that every year shall be renewed the praises of those among our national geniuses who have so distinguished themselves as to be most deserving in the three divine arts of design.

To-day, since this august temple of the Muses is more resplendent than ever, he should not presume to attempt fulfilling this noble office who but imperfectly knows and under-

* See Note O

[179]

stands their alluring graces As for me, to come forth as
little ingloriously as possible from this difficult undertaking,
I intend to devote my efforts to another object, and I trust
that I shall see your courtesy smile upon me, if, leaving aside
pencil, rule, and chisel, I look rather toward those who
protect artists, and call your attention to a most remarkable
Mæcenas * I shall thus, overcoming any excessive timidity,
be able to entertain you a little regarding the advantages
which students of the Academy may derive from this kind of
tutelage, and I shall present to you, in his proper light, a
great man of the sixteenth century who belonged to the order
of the Venetian patriciate.

LOUIS CORNARO is known to all cultured nations by
the famous abstemiousness of his long career and by the
golden rules he formulated concerning the temperate life,
but it is not perhaps so well known how deeply versed he was
in the arts, how much he loved artists, and how faithfully he
labored in their interest. I shall speak now of these merits
of his, and I shall do it with the rapidity of a hasty traveler
who does but lightly observe and examine If I turn my eyes
upon Cornaro in preference to so many other great men, who,
for the good of the arts, were nurtured upon these shores, I
trust the choice will be approved; since it will bear upon a
subject honorable to our fellow-citizens, pleasing to our
worthy professors, useful to these valiant youths—one which
may, in fine, be heard patiently by every kind and gentle soul

Of the youthful years of our Cornaro, spent in Padua,
there is little to say, and that little were better left unsaid
Although well trained in excellent studies, as became a gentleman of fine intellect, he admits that he soon put his studies
aside, and wasted his time in thoughtlessness and excesses;
from which cause he contracted infirm health and such bad
habits that, having arrived at the age of thirty-five, he had
nothing left to hope for but that he might end in death the
sufferings of a worn-out and disconsolate life. Let us not
linger, my dear young men, over this state of affairs, which,
happily, we shall soon see corrected; but let us learn, by his

* See Note P

[180]

example, how important it is to follow the straight path of virtue and study Though the contrary way of dissipation and idleness may seem, to some, to be one of peace and calmness, in reality it is nothing but war and storm

When he had grown ripe in years and judgment, his inborn love having unfolded toward those sister arts which are the dearest ornaments of our native land, Cornaro found in them the truest, most useful, and most delightful entertainment. Let us listen to the substance of his words: "O most honorable gentlemen, great in intellect, in manners, and in letters, and you who excel in some other quality, come with me to honor the arts and artists, and, in doing so, obtain satisfaction and comfort! .. I live in the most beautiful part of this noble and learned city of Padua, and derive from it a thousand advantages. I build according to architecture, enjoy my several gardens, and always find something to delight me. . In April and May, as also in September and October, I find other pleasures in enjoying a country-seat of mine among the Euganean Hills,—in the finest site thereof,—with its fountains and gardens, and, above all, its commodious and beautiful abode; also my villa in the plain, which is very fine, with streets and a square, and a church much honored , . a country, which, once deserted on account of bad air and marshy waters, is now, by my labors, all rich in inhabitants and fields most fertile; so that I may say, with truth, that in this spot I have given to God an altar, a temple, and souls to adore Him....Here I take pleasure with men of fine intellect— architects, painters, sculptors, musicians, and agriculturists; for, indeed, with such men our age is abundantly furnished "

And you well know, gentlemen, how fruitful that age was in fine minds. Happy age! Private individuals vied with noblemen and princes to rejoice the heavens with splendid light; and, thanks to this union of choice spirits, the genius of Italy was aroused, literature came to the fore, the arts thrived, and a refined delicacy was diffused into every liberal study. Let us not stir from this incomparable Venice of ours and we will see that, if her noblest citizens—a Daniel Barbaro, a Cardinal Bembo, a Doge Gritti, a Cardinal Grimani, a

Giorgio Trissino of Vicenza, and our own Cornaro—had not lived, the world would perhaps have never seen a Titian, a Paolo [Veronese], a Sammicheli, a Palladio. How many, indeed, are the opportunities of an intelligent protector! Besides showing himself liberal of his substance, he converses with his learned friend, whose inventions and fancies are thus fostered, he goes to the office of the rich merchant, into whom he transfuses the enthusiasm with which he himself is filled,... nor does he neglect any occasion whatsoever that the arts may gloriously flourish In Greece, the mother of all elegance and philosophy, the Porticos and the Piræus became earth and brambles, once the ages of Pericles and Alexander were past; and in earth and brambles the Laocoon and the Apollo for centuries lay buried

Among the many artists for whom Cornaro entertained a strong affection,—proofs of which he has left us,—I shall limit myself to telling you of one. Giovanni Maria Falconetto* of Verona, who excelled as painter, architect, and sculptor, flourished in his day. This man was a good speaker, frank and pleasant; and, after having wandered hither and thither, he found a refuge in the hospitable home of our Cornaro, who offered him the most generous recognition. These two souls were soon united in close fellowship; and there followed many learned and agreeable conversations, and the most valued friendship and intimacy

A large collection of drawings, which Falconetto had brought with him from Rome, so fascinated Cornaro with the attractions of that queenly city that he insisted upon going to visit it, in company with his friend. He departed for Rome, rich in expectations; most rich in knowledge, he returned to his beloved Padua. There he erected a magnificent loggia, decorated it with paintings, statues, and pictures taken from the designs of Raphael, and inclosed in its courtyard a most noble casino, devoted to music—all under the superintendence and according to the directions of his friend Falconetto. He also availed himself of his assistance in other grand constructions at his villa at Codovico, on the Paduan hill, and at Luigiano, near Torreglia, among the Euganean Hills. Nor

* See Note E

[182]

did the happy alliance between the Mæcenas and the artist ever cease; and the latter was comforted at his death by the assurance that the most hospitable kindness would ever be lavished upon his wife, three sons, and six daughters, the fortunes of all of whom remained, in fact, at the mercy of the credit and authority of their patron and friend   The candid soul of Louis bore so great a predilection to Falconetto and another happy mind, the Paduan Ruzzante,* that Vasari has related, in his works, how Cornaro wished that Falconetto and Ruzzante should be buried together, and that he might be the third to share the same grave—in order that (says the historian) "not even after death should their bodies be separated, whose souls friendship and virtue had united whilst living."

I have pointed out some of the edifices designed and erected by Cornaro; and it will be pleasing to you, gentlemen, if I remind you that the magnificent loggia raised in Padua is still in existence and much admired, and that the very celebrated architect Sebastiano Serlio proposed the designs of this masterpiece to the studious as a model worthy of imitation. Temanza, in his account of the life of Falconetto, also speaks to us, at length, of the buildings erected in the villa at Codovico, where he still found remains of perfect invention and execution, it was there he discovered a portrait of our most honored Mæcenas, one that I should like to see decorating this magnificent hall on this solemn occasion in which I am striving to recall his deeds   Temanza was not well informed when speaking to us of the palace at Luigiano, which he believed had been built near the Sile, not far from the city of Trevigio, and razed by time; but to the culture and knowledge of the illustrious Knight Giovanni de Lazzara, I owe—and you do, likewise—the pleasing news that this structure, with its truly royal stairways, remains standing in that most delightful spot I have spoken of among the Euganean Hills. It has become the property of the famous Bishopric of Padua, and does not belie the estimate given of it in his day by our Francesco Marcolini, who, in one of his dedications, wrote thus· "If a gentleman wishes to learn how to build in the

* See Note Q

[183]

city, let him come to the Cornaro Palace at Padua.... If he wishes to lay out a garden, let him also find his model there   If he wants to build in the country, let him go and see at Codovico, at Campagna, and at other places, the structures created by the nobility of Cornaro's great soul. .. If he wants to build a palace fit for a prince,—out of the city, too,—let him go to Luvignano, where he will behold a dwelling worthy to be inhabited by a pontiff or an emperor; .. Cornaro knows all there is to know in this and in the rest of human undertakings." Note, my hearers, that the engraver Marcolini was no ordinary man, but was indeed a most famous artist, and so skilled in the mechanical sciences that he was praised to the skies by Daniel Barbaro himself.

And here I wish to interrupt my narrative a while to listen to you, gentlemen, who take pleasure in considering the things which I propound. It seems to me you would wish to rejoin: "Granted, that thy Cornaro was the mirror of Mæcenases—and who does not know that to them the arts owe both favor and increase? and we may add that they owed these same things at one time to the majesty of religion, now enfeebled,. and also to many men of wealth grown poor to-day Let a Cornaro return now, and with him a Titian and a Paolo, let the artists return in throngs,— what of it? Poor father of a family, thou dost spend, and indeed waste, for that son of thine who is now a studious scholar in this Academy, but who runs the risk of remaining afterward destitute, without bread and without fortune! Poor boy, thou burnest the midnight oil in the sweat of thy brow, but in the future thou wilt, perforce, be inactive; and it would be wrong to dare thee to the field of valor, where there will be no palms to gather when thou hast attained thy end!"

I shall not invoke the shade of the Venetian Mæcenas to answer similar whisperings, for, if our times are not his, it is to ours we must conform. I wish to say, however, that many unfounded difficulties proceed from vain fears. If religion, the comforter, seems to have become feeble, or to have lost its power with some, the neglect of a few is not a fault to be laid to the many; and all know that a society without religion is like a ship without rudder or sails. Do we not see it burning bravely in the hearts of our ruler and so many of his excellent magistrates, burning in the honored breasts of the best of our citizens; burning in the bosoms of noble matrons and of the humble peasant girls? And you need but enter the churches to see the solemn services always attended by throngs of people, or to journey through the country to witness respect and veneration everywhere manifested.

It is only too true that the murderous weapons from beyond the hills, catching us unarmed, deprived us of a great part of our riches; and, alas! too often now the oak stands bare which used to tower in vigor. But, perhaps, rather than to the lukewarmness of divine worship or the swords of the enemy, we might attribute to other causes the scarcity of work among our artists. It is incessantly repeated that we have become poor; but how is it, then, that there is immoderate luxury in all that regards outward pomp? that an Indian fabric, a bit of Sèvres porcelain, a piece of Birmingham earthenware, the gold and silver spun in France or Germany, and many other useless but costly trifles from foreign countries, never lie dusty in our shops, while the hands of our artists are idle? Pray do not lead me to exclaim that there is among us more poverty concerning the true love of our country's splendor, than poverty of goods.

The conditions of modern Italy would with difficulty give us back a Cornaro, but there must be other means for the protection of the arts, even without so much power as his.

This Adria of ours is no longer, such as the illustrious Roberti depicted it, "Like to the ancient Tyre, whose navigators were her Phœnicians; when its commerce, which raised up the towers and halls of the lagoons, at the same time made the country everywhere populous and honored." Nevertheless, for an active Mæcenas of the arts, an earnest magistrate is often sufficient; frequently one enlightened citizen is enough, or the wise pastor of a church; and, indeed, we see active Mæcenases in not a few of the latter, who, in

[185]

the midst of rural surroundings, erect magnificent temples
enriched in many ways. By enthusiasm, intelligence, and
activity, we shall see our buildings repaired and beautified,
and our houses more properly decorated with the riches of our
national productions—thus, in a word, our cities ennobled.
Call to mind, gentlemen, that through the activity and fervor
of one of our pastors in these latter days, the temple of Santi
Giovanni e Paolo has been transformed into a magnificent
gallery; that the worthy Knight Morelli has there rearranged
and enriched, with many relics of the fine arts, a library, the
most splendid abode Apollo and Minerva could have; that the
Prefect of the Seminary, Giannantonio Moschini, has converted a dilapidated building into a magnificent and ornate
lyceum, that our most illustrious President, whom I name
not to flatter but to honor, and who is always intent upon
honorable undertakings which nourish the arts and carry
their teachings to the farthest shores, has obtained for you
from our rulers the means by which this Academy now ranks
above all others   Seeing all this, let us rejoice and take comfort—you especially, most learned professors. Rejoice that
you are the fortunate ministers who maintain here the sacred
fire of the divine works of the intellect, and know all that is
exquisite and hidden in their structure. Take comfort in the
names of...many who were once your scholars and who are
now the solace and help of their families, their brows wreathed
with crowns of honor woven for them by your teachings.
And you, dearest youths, who are this day prepared to receive
new and much-desired laurels, never pay heed to the reports
spread by ignoble fear, but redouble your earnestness in study;
and you will thus become the delight of your friends and the
honor of your country.

Let us return now to Louis Cornaro, and follow him in
what we may of his long life; nor let us abandon him until its
last day Oh, how I wish the chroniclers had been less
niggardly to us! For, history having passed over in silence
so many of the personal acts of that gentle spirit, we cannot
now know positively either all his works or many of his
writings; but must be content with the little we have, which,

like the plan of a majestic building, suffices only to make us guess at the grandeur of the structure and the splendor of its decorations. The few letters which remain to us from his pen, show how well versed he was in every noble science; and, being addressed to great men, such as Bembo, Speroni, Barbaro, and Fracastoro, they suffice to show of what excellence were his ties of friendship He left nothing undone that would promote intellectual enjoyment. The celebrated tragedy, "Œdipus," by Giovanni Andrea dell' Anguillara, he caused to be sumptuously presented under his own roof for the recreation of the Paduans The "Canace" of Speroni was also to have been given in Padua with singular magnificence, and to our Louis was entrusted the direction of the performance Forcellini, in his biography of Speroni, relates that Cornaro's companions in this were Alessandro Piccolomini and Angelo Beolco, called Ruzzante; and that, besides having provided music, costumes, and luxurious scenery for the beauty of the performance, he had prepared a great banquet for forty chosen gentlewomen and their husbands, the academicians and the flower of the men of merit who were at that time in Padua; but the unexpected death of Ruzzante put an end to all these plans. Finally, we know how deeply he had studied the works of Vitruvius and Leon Battista Alberti; and that he was much praised by Andrea Palladio, as the inventor of a new kind of stairway introduced into his habitations. Nor is that all, for he dictated various treatises concerning painting, architecture, music, and agriculture. But the only writings which were not destroyed by time, are the discourses upon his cherished temperate life—translations of which were published in many foreign tongues—and a learned pamphlet upon our lagoons, which he used to style "the most strong and holy ramparts" of his dear country

I, who like to borrow the words of the aged, which breathe candor and simplicity and add faith to speech, beg you to hear with me how a cultured Tuscan man of letters, Antonmaria Graziani, in the life he wrote of the celebrated Commendone,—whose secretary he was,—points out the many blessings which our Cornaro was in the habit of receiving from the virtuous temper of his soul His words are in the Latin tongue, and this is their import in ours: "This most honorable man, whom the surname of Temperate became so well, was courted, revered, and respected by all, whether those of eminent birth or those distinguished by great intellect, and men of all ranks of society were eager to visit him, for the pleasure of hearing his conversation, which was always moderate, pleasant, and ingenious Prudence, wisdom, sagacity, counsel, and liberality formed about him a most beautiful and splendid body-guard No house in Padua was more looked up to than his; and he, always magnificent and bountiful, never ceased to bestow upon all—but, in an especial manner, upon those conversant with the fine arts— every favor of a generous and perfect soul". .

But I shall lead you at length, gentlemen, to the last days of Louis Cornaro, and it will be sweet to you to know that to spend one's time unceasingly for the common good is to lay up precious consolation for the last hour of our lives And here I shall again make use of Graziani's words, that you may see how the tranquil and restful end of our great man. was as serene as the beautiful sunset of an unclouded day. "The good old man" (I follow the faithful translation) "feeling that he drew near the end, did not look upon the great transit with fear, but as though he were about to pass from one house into another. He was seated in his little bed —he used a small and very narrow one, and, at its side, was his wife, Veronica, almost his equal in years. In a clear and sonorous voice he told me why he would be able to leave this life with a valiant soul, and he expressed the best wishes for the happiness of my Commendone, to whom he insisted upon writing with his own hand a letter of advice and consolation. He told me he thought he might yet survive two days; but, feeling a little later the failure of vital forces, and having received anew the assistance of consoling religion, .. he exclaimed: 'Glad and full of hope will I go with you, my good God!' He then composed himself, and having closed his eyes, as though about to sleep, with a slight sigh he left us forever." A departure joyful and enviable, but how great a misfortune to the world! For the loss of men of so great wisdom is irreparable; nor is anything left to us but to follow, as far as may be, their authority and example. ...

Dear and noble youths, this solemnity is sacred chiefly to you; and, addressing you, I shall close my discourse. With the voice of warmest affection, I urge you to be industrious in winning for yourselves the patronage of the prince and the assistance of the Mæcenas, and never again to forget Louis Cornaro and the artist Falconetto, his friend. Yes, to-day also you will find protectors, if, having made for yourselves a treasure of all domestic virtues, you broaden the sphere of your intellect with a great variety of knowledge, and if you will bear in mind that he does not win fame and celebrity who is slothful, but rather does he who works night and day, so far as human nature will permit. Livy and Plutarch have described for us Philopœmen, an illustrious leader of armies, and have narrated the great labors and efforts which bore him to celebrity. Reynolds set that general as an example before his young scholars, and showed them that not less arduous are the labors and efforts of the artist who would ascend the heights of immortality. Therefore, we all trust to your talent and good-will, and by you, valiant youths, this city will continually rise to greater luster; which, for delightfulness of climate, vividness of genius, holiness of institutions, majesty and splendor of buildings, and for the purest milk afforded the three divine sister arts, has ever been famous throughout the whole world.

"O flowerets of the field!" Siddârtha said,
"Who turn your tender faces to the sun,—
Glad of the light, and grateful with sweet breath
Of fragrance and these robes of reverence donned,
Silver and gold and purple,—none of ye
Miss perfect living, none of ye despoil
Your happy beauty.   O ye palms! which rise
Eager to pierce the sky and drink the wind
Blown from Malaya and the cool blue seas;
What secret know ye that ye grow content,
From time of tender shoot to time of fruit,
Murmuring such sun-songs from your feathered crowns?"

—Sir Edwin Arnold.

THE VILLAS

ERECTED BY LOUIS CORNARO

BY

DR. PROF. EMILIO LOVARINI *

OF THE

REALE LICEO MINGHETTI OF
BOLOGNA **

FAMOUS for his treatise, "The Temperate Life," which
has not only been translated into several languages, but
has seen many editions, the illustrious Venetian gentleman, Louis Cornaro, deserves imperishable renown, likewise,
for the great and useful love which he bore for the arts—
particularly for architecture

"He delighted," we have from Serlio, "in all the noble
arts and singular attainments, and especially was he fond of
architecture" It was in the latter that he acquired his title
to undying fame, as even his contemporaries acknowledged.
Among these was Ortensio Lando, who, wishing to praise
him, made this merit precede all others when he called him
"a great builder, an enthusiastic hunter, and a man of pro-
found piety."

* See Note R
** From Vol II , Nos. VI.-VII ,—April-July 1899,—of "L'Arte" of Rome

[191]

Architecture was not for him, as it is for so many, purely
a luxury, and a means by which he could exhibit his riches
to the envious and wondering eyes of his equals, and of the
world in general   Rather was it the object of an ardent worship ; so much so that he became not only a friend, but even
a helper and companion, of his artist protégés.

He studied the works of Vitruvius, Leon Battista Alberti,
and other writers, and visited the ancient and modern architectural monuments, he originated, according to Palladio,
"two kinds of stairways"; and he composed a work on
architecture, which a relative of his, in a letter dated January
27, 1554, insisted should be published, but nothing came of it,
and it has never been known.

Fortunately, instead of a treatise on the subject, he left
something better to us, in the form of several very handsome buildings.   Much more would he have left had his
means allowed it; for, as Vasari writes, "He was a man of
great genius and of a truly regal spirit—the truth of this
statement being proved by so many of his honored undertakings."   This opinion is perfectly in accord with that of
Pietro Valeriano, who, in a Latin dedication of a work to
Cornaro, wrote. "To-day, no private individual understands
better than you the science, beauty, and elegance of construction, or has more artistically turned his knowledge to practical
use.   Had, perchance, a destiny worthy of your great soul
befallen you, our age would be considered inferior to no
ancient one in the development of such a noble art"

What he did accomplish, however, is undoubtedly well
worthy of being recorded.   The ingenious Francesco Marcolini, an expert printer and artist, and designer of the bridge
"whence Murano watches Venice," was the first and last to
prepare a list, which is thus the only one we have, of Cornaro's
buildings

One finds this list in a letter, dated June 1, 1544, in which
the editor,—Marcolini,—dedicating to Cornaro the fourth
book of Serlio, writes: "To you alone can one give the
name of 'executor' of true architecture, as is attested by the

[192]

splendid edifices ordered by your superhuman intellect. If a nobleman or private gentleman wishes to know how to build in a city, let him come to the Cornaro Palace at Padua; there he will learn how to construct not only a superb portico, but also the other parts of sumptuous and comfortable buildings. If he wishes to adorn a garden, let him take, as a model, the one you have arranged, not only under your dwelling, but crossing beneath the highroad for twenty paces—all in rustic style. If he is desirous of building in the country, let him go to Codevigo, to Campagna, and to the other places where he will find the buildings which are the product of your great genius. Whoever wishes to build a princely palace—also away from the city—may go to Luvignano, there he will view, with astonishment, a mansion worthy of a pope or an emperor, or, at any rate, of any prelate or gentleman—a mansion erected by the wisdom of your Excellency, who knows all that is possible in this and other human achievements."

With all the exaggerations to be noted in the laudatory expressions of those times, Cornaro is by Marcolini called merely the "executor" of true architecture, this does not mean that he was the author of all those magnificent edifices, but rather that they were "ordered" by him, as is added later on

It ought to have been known even in that time—as Vasari tells us, though it is omitted above—that, even if Cornaro was the architect of his palace in Padua, "the beautiful and richly ornamented portico," close by, was the work of the skillful Falconetto*—a fact which is also mentioned in the inscription existing above the central archway. It should, moreover, be remembered that Falconetto "worked a great deal with the said Cornaro." Without further proofs, and without any documents, we think it quite useless at the present day to try to discover, by the examination of the architectural style alone of what remains, how much is the work of the one and how much that of the other. Equally devoted to classical art, they lived together twenty-one years in an uninterrupted unison of feelings and ideas, so much so, that

* See Note E

[193]

Cornaro expressed a wish that he might be buried in one tomb with his friend—"so that their bodies might not be separated in death, whose souls in this world had been united by friendship and virtue."

With these facts before us, it does not seem right to accept the opinion of some, who, like Temanza, see Falconetto's work wherever Cornaro has built; or that of others who attribute all to Cornaro; but, until further proof is attainable, it would be wise to abstain from giving any positive opinion.

The portico, together with other parts of the city palace, has been described and commended by many; and, though it is not widely known, there are always foreigners who visit it. But who goes to visit the edifices mentioned by Marcolini, and the others omitted by him, all away from the city? Not only has very little been written about them, but some of them have, unfortunately, been forever lost.

Last summer, while traveling through the Venetian country, I went to the scenes of Cornaro's work, to find how much had, by time and man, been left of the buildings. I did not find all that he had built, or even all that had been seen by some writers at the end of the last century; but I clearly saw that what yet remains is well worth illustrating and writing about. Among these remains is a fine architectural work, which, until now, so far as I am able to learn, had been forgotten; I also found some useful documents in the course of my researches in the archives. Therefore, uniting the fruits of my two investigations, I deemed it well to make known what I have myself learned about the works constructed in the country by the illustrious nobleman.

It is well, from the very first, to make a distinction between the edifices built at Cornaro's own expense and for his own use, and those built by him for the account of Cardinal Francesco Pisani,—Bishop of Padua from 1524 to 1567,—for whom Cornaro acted as administrator during several years. The distinction is readily made; for there still remain the documents relating to Cornaro's property, which had been presented at different times to the officials of the Commune of Padua. They do not register any property at either Campagna or Luvigliano Here, therefore, his work was for the Bishopric and not for himself. Let us now commence with these two places

At Campagna Lupia, near Dolo, not very far from the lagoon, is a large farmhouse which belonged to the Bishop of Padua, but is now owned by a gentleman of that city. It was this house that Temanza recognized as the one mentioned by Marcolini as Cornaro's work; though he arbitrarily put it to the credit of Falconetto, and published it as such in his biographical work, in 1778.

Twenty-four years later, it was visited by the publisher Pietro Brandolese, a passionate lover of artistic researches relating to Venice, who described it minutely in an unpublished letter to Count Giovanni de Lazzara, as follows: "At a short distance from the church, or rather just before coming to it, is a country-house belonging to the Bishopric of Padua, built by Falconetto It is the same one to which Temanza refers, at page 138 and the following pages, under the simple denomination of 'seventeen arches ' It is wholly of a rustic style, built of brick and carefully selected stone The façade is formed of seventeen arches of slight proportions, flanked by very strong pillars There is no aperture whatever above these, and the façade ends with a simple band which serves as a cornice Under the portico the building is divided into three parts by two stairways which lead to the granaries, the central section receding a little from the sides. Without a plan before us, it is not possible to describe the arrangement of the ground floor, which possesses every convenience for farming purposes: rooms for the peasants; stables for cattle, horses, and all kinds of animals , cellars , etc., —all very cleverly arranged. The vaults are wholly in brick —not beams On the first floor are the granaries, which one can enter by the stairs, as well as from the terraces by means

[195]

of an arched bridge, as is clearly seen by what remains near the courtyard door This door, in rustic style, is nearly all lost The façade of the portico is all of hewn stone, with apertures cleverly arranged, corresponding to the uses of the house and to its internal disposition. The entire building, in fact, gives evidence of a very skillful architect Its plans would serve, to-day, as an ingenious model for a farmhouse, with due allowance, however, for all the modern needs which differ from those of that age."

The Count de Lazzara, fifteen years later, in a letter which was published by Gamba, warrants the statement that Cornaro had "presided" over the construction of this farmhouse, and that its architect was his guest. But not even Bishop Dondi Orologio, who had made researches for him among the old documents, had been able to find the name of this architect, or of any other. Wherefore he wrote thus "If Temanza speaks of the beautiful portico at Campagna as having been built by Louis Cornaro, the author of 'The Temperate Life,' I doubt his being right. Cornaro was the administrator of the Bishopric of Padua for many years, and, under the date of August 17, 1546, there is a writing of Cardinal Pisani, in which the Bishop admits owing the aforesaid Cornaro 11,120 ducats, for buildings and improvements made by him on the property of the Bishopric. The document does not say where the buildings were, nor where the improvements were made, perhaps, among the former, the one at Campagna is included "

The learned Bishop was wise in presuming only that which was likely, and affirming nothing more. If it is probable that Falconetto may have had something to do with it, there are no proofs; so it is useless to mention his name We may, indeed, believe that the building was erected during Cornaro's administration, and the fact of its having been attributed to him since 1544, in a letter publicly addressed to him, ought to be more than sufficient proof. Under such circumstances, doubt is unreasonable.

Certain documents, regarding the adjustment of the

accounts of Cornaro and Cardinal Pisani, testify that the illustrious administrator was occupied, during the years 1532, '33, and '34, in establishing throughout the lands of the Bishopric the system of farming on equal shares; and an eye-witness tells us that "at Campagna his ambitions in this regard were fully realized." In all likelihood that was the time when the necessity for some large place in which to store the harvest was most felt, and Cornaro must have provided for it by building the country-house in question. There are, in fact, records of an account for stone used in building the barns at Campagna, which account was presented to the Cardinal. The place was commonly called "the granary of Campagna," and it was also designated "the episcopal palace in the domain of Campagna" It is, to-day, in much the same condition as described by Brandolese

Not very far from the monumental Abbey of Praglia—upon a little eminence at the foot of the Euganean Hills, from which one commands the view of a great part of the Paduan plain—rises the palace at Luvigliano, to which ascent is gained from the east and west by superb double stairways This was probably the site of the old village church and parish house which were demolished and built elsewhere, in 1474, at the expense of Bishop Jacobo Zeno, to make way, perhaps, for the new building and the adjacent gardens. At all events, the palace was erected and completed much later by Cornaro—as Marcolini tells us—and, consequently, during his administration, indications, indeed, are not wanting to confirm this view.

In the documents pertaining to the adjustment already alluded to, this palace at Luvigliano is likewise mentioned in reference to the stone employed, as well as to other building expenses It is also likely that when Cornaro gave up his care of the Bishopric's property the palace was already completed, as would appear from the allusion referring to it, found in a summary of his administration "and he completed the work which he had begun "

Later, during the incumbency of Francesco and Alvise

Pisani,—prior to 1570,—the fine doorways leading into the park and courtyard, the fountain, the crenelated battlements, and other things of more or less secondary importance, were constructed by the architect Andrea Da Valle, the sculptor Agostino Righetti, and others. In the course of time occurred other small additions or restorations; but always in conformity with the original design of the villa, in which one can admire, to this day, the happy intellect that created it.

This, like the rest of Cornaro's buildings, has been attributed to his friend without any proof or reason. Selvatico alone reasoned, after examining the palace, that "The style of architecture, more than any of the historical notes, discloses it to be the work of Falconetto"; and he added this opinion: "Though not everyone may be contented with all that adorns this structure, none can help admiring the beauty and richness of its design."

Great astonishment was felt that Cardinal Francesco Pisani visited only once—perhaps in 1547, and just for a few hours—that superb and exquisite palace which used to fill with pride the hearts even of those who had merely the good fortune to own property in its neighborhood; as was the case with that chaplain who wrote, in Latin, this inscription on the wall.

"LANGFRANCUS CANIPANONA, NICKNAMED LIGNEAMINEUS, THE SON OF ALEXANDER, CHAPLAIN OF THE CHURCH OF THE FATHER, HAS PREPARED THIS HOUSE, TOGETHER WITH THE ADJOINING HILL CAREFULLY CULTIVATED BY HIM AND COVERING FIFTEEN FIELDS, NEAR THE VERY BEAUTIFUL PALACE AND DELIGHTFUL GARDENS OF THE BISHOPRIC, IN THE VILLAGE OF LIVIANUS, FOR PLEASURE AND FOR THE CONVENIENCE OF HIS FRIENDS, IN THE YEAR MDLXIII."

In one of his dialogues, published in 1561, the eminent jurist, Marco Mantova Benavides, puts these words in the mouth of Ulisse Bassiani: "You certainly do the place [the suburban villa at Bassanello] a wrong no less than does Cardinal Pisani, who has only been once to the palace which he has constructed at Covigliano [*sic*] at such an enormous expense that it commands the admiration of all who see it; and even then he did not remain more than a day." Oh, what were the quiet pleasures of a residence in such a place, to the ambition of a Cardinal who was eligible to the papal chair! He abandoned even his Bishopric for Rome!

Louis Cornaro, on the other hand, knew how to, and did, find such pleasures; and all the things he had built for himself he enjoyed both heartily and for a great length of time. In 1542, remembering that he had always benefited "literati, musicians, architects, painters, sculptors, and others," and that he had spent "many and many thousands of crowns in stately buildings and in many beautiful gardens," to Speroni he prided himself that he knew how to enjoy every happiness in "such well-arranged habitations and beautiful gardens of his own creation." And, though "many who attain these things do not generally enjoy them," he promised himself that, thanks to his temperate life, he would yet continue to enjoy them many and many years—which promise he certainly fulfilled. Later, in his happy and industrious old age, he again expressed his satisfaction over it; and he delighted to tell how he divided his time between town and country. To this very circumstance we are indebted to him for some interesting points on the subject of our research.

"I go." he writes, "in April and May, and again in September and October, to enjoy a country-seat of mine in the Euganean Hills, most beautifully situated, with its gardens and fountains, and especially its beautiful and comfortable dwelling. I sometimes go there, also, to take part in the pleasant and agreeable hunting, of the kind suitable to my age. I enjoy, for as many days, my villa in the plain, which is beautiful, with many pretty streets all meeting in a fine square, in the center of which stands its church, highly honored, as befits the importance of the place. The villa is divided by a wide and rapid branch of the river Brenta, on

either side of which the country extends in cultivated and
fertile fields, and it is now—the Lord be thanked!—very well
populated, which before was certainly not the case, but rather
the opposite, as it was marshy and malarial, and more suited
to snakes than to men. After I had drained off the water, the
air became pure, and people began to settle; the inhabitants
multiplied greatly, and the place grew to the perfect state
in which one sees it to-day. I can, therefore, truly say that
in this place I gave to God an altar, a temple, and souls to
worship Him."

This is the village of Codevigo, about four miles distant
from Piove di Sacco; here the records of the Paduan Commune indicate, in addition to the numerous and extensive
possessions of Cornaro, a house for his own use, "with a
courtyard, kitchen-garden, orchard, and vineyard" of about
the size of "five fields." One of his nephews, in a letter,
describes it as follows: "His country-seat, both comfortable
and adapted to agriculture, is built according to the finest
architecture, and is stronger and more commodious than any
other in the neighborhood. He wished to construct the vaults
entirely of stone, so as to be safe in case of fire, war, or any
other calamity." Marcolini also confirms that it was built by
Cornaro.

In the same village,—according to this nephew,—besides
the beautiful church which he transformed from the un-
attractive structure it had formerly been, and the altar of
which Cornaro himself spoke, he also built the bridge over the
river Brenta—"a work worthy not only of a single individual
but of a whole community"—as well as many houses for the
farmers. But, in the course of time, much of all this was lost,
and there remains, at present, even less than was seen by
Temanza and Brandolese.

Temanza, who always returned gladly to those places to
see Cornaro's edifices, which he judged as "works of merit
and worthy of being imitated," wrote in the following manner: "At the village of Codevigo in the country round Padua,
situated on the right bank of the river Brenta,—which, in that

part, is called Brentone,—Cornaro owned an enormous estate.
The health of the place was impaired by stagnant waters, for
the drainage of which no means had as yet been provided, and
he, who for those times was learned in hydrostatics, reduced the
marshes to dry land, improved the condition of the atmosphere,
and thereby caused a great increase in the number of settlers.
He first built the parish church, dedicated to the prophet
Zacharias. He then constructed a noble, though not very
large, palace, with porticos and courtyards, as becomes a villa.
All these buildings are the work of Giovanni Maria [Fal-
conetto]. A majestic doorway forms the entrance to the
palace. It has two Ionic columns on the sides, a rich cornice,
and a majestic frontispiece, which bears, carved in the center
of its upper part, a large eagle with wings outspread This
edifice has two stories, the first is vaulted, the second has
rafted ceilings The lower part of the church façade,—which
is in Doric style,—as well as the doorway and windows,
reminds one of the style of Falconetto. The altar bears the
same character, and has a fine terra-cotta bas-relief of good
workmanship, representing a scene in the life of the prophet
Zacharias."

One cannot imagine where Temanza obtained his information about the priority of the building of the church, or
the certainty that all these edifices were due to Falconetto,
though his writings are decidedly of value, for, as early as
1802, vandal hands had begun to destroy these monuments.

As good fortune would have it, in that very year, on the
eighth of July, Brandolese happened to be there, and he gave
to Count de Lazzara the following narrative of his experience·
"I proceeded eagerly to Codevigo, to learn what remained
there of Falconetto's work The church does not exist any
more, except, as you know, the Doric part of the façade, and
of these remains I admired the model and the elegance of
different parts On entering the church to see the altar, I
found that the place where it used to exist was in the course
of reconstruction, and saw the original pieces thrown care-
lessly on the ground I inquired what was to be the fate of

this fine monument, and learned that it was to be reduced and refitted for a new chapel. I pleaded with the parish priest that it might be rebuilt as it was originally, and I trust I have obtained the favor. I observed the archway in the buildings close by, now belonging to the Foscari family, and I admired more than ever the wise investigator of the remains of Roman art."

Brandolese's words were heeded, and the exquisite altar remains to this day, though without the table and the terracotta bas-relief; and it occupies the chapel to the left of the principal altar

The old bridge, and the doorway of the Cornaro Palace, however, exist no longer. The building has been repeatedly modified, and now presents nothing especially worthy of notice; only a few stones, which may have formed the base of the columns of the doorway, still lie scattered about under the courtyard portico The façade of the church, which is Doric below and Corinthian above, had been recently whitened; and the old steeple, which leaned so greatly to one side as to threaten a collapse, had been supported with a buttress extending nearly to the belfry

We have yet to speak of the other villa mentioned by Cornaro before he spoke of Codevigo He does not name it, but only says it was in the Euganean Hills and "in their most beautiful spot." Some thought of Luvigliano, and supposed that he had there taken to draining the marshes, felling the woods, breaking up the ground, and cultivating the lands; and they said that the fact of his having breathed the pure air of that place was one of the causes which prolonged his life to a very old age Gamba believed that it did not become the property of the Bishopric of Padua until sometime later; but such, as we have seen, it had always been; and we cannot believe that the noble Cornaro considered it, even during his administration, as his own property, or lived there as if it were his own home. Of which place, then, does he mean to speak?

Not one of the many who have written about him has ever yet told us, notwithstanding the fact that in 1842, among the collection of Venetian inscriptions edited by Cicogna, was published the letter of Cornaro's nephew, already mentioned, which explains that this villa was at Este.

"He created," writes the nephew, "on a hill near Este, a delightful garden, full of divers and delicate fountains and perfect grapes" And, continuing: "In his youth he delighted in hunting big game, such as wild boar and the stag; and, as such animals were not to be found in this country [near Padua], but in the territory of Este divided by an arm of the Po [sic], he built there a comfortable hunting residence; and annually, for many a year, he used to go there, killing a large number of these animals, which he either sent to some of his friends, or else distributed in Venice or Padua. When the sport was at its end, he had a comedy prepared and given in his own hall, which he had built in imitation of the ancient ones. The stage was made of durable stone, but the part reserved for the audience was of wood, so that it could be taken down and removed These performances were all very successful, as he had living with him some clever artists, such as the famous *Ruzzante."

Furthermore, the Paduan records confirm, without any doubt, that he owned "a house on the hills outside the gates of Este, with an orchard and a vineyard of six fields," which he kept for his private use

Carefully examining all the records, as well as all the histories of Este that have ever been published, I found—and that in a monograph of 1851—only the following uncertain allusion to a Cornaro Villa built at that place: "Beyond [the Kunkler Palace] to the left, is a palace, perhaps in old days that of Cornaro, and later belonging to the Farsetti family; it is built on a beautiful height, and has been, according to the designs of Japelli, enlarged and improved with great taste by its present owner, Doctor Adolfo Benvenuti"

I then went to Este to find this Villa Benvenuti; and, to my surprise and delight, I found at the entrance of the garden

* See Note Q

[203]

a fine archway of classic style, in which I thought I saw no little resemblance to the architectural works of Cornaro and Falconetto The situation of the villa coincides precisely with the description in the records of Padua, for we find, by examining old topographical maps, that, in order to get to it from the center of the city, it was necessary to pass the Santa Tecla gate, which was demolished centuries ago

The archives of the city of Este contained nothing that could convert my supposition into certainty, but a few days later, while examining the old papers of the Bishopric of Padua, I came upon a contract of 1650, in which the Procurator Giovanni Battista Cornaro had leased to Giorgio Cornaro, Bishop of Padua, for ten years, "his palace at Este, near the convent of the Capuchins, with all its fields, kitchen-gardens, orchards, parks, fountains, vineyards, etc" To this contract was annexed a minutely detailed inventory of the furniture in the house. This document dispelled all my doubts, as many details mentioned in it are identical with the views of the Villa Farsetti and its garden, drawn by Coronelli in the beginning of the eighteenth century, and other particulars have been preserved. and are noticeable to this day, in the Villa Benvenuti. This villa, belonging formerly to the Farsetti family, is therefore none other than the old Villa Cornaro it is near the convent of the Capuchins, and nearer to it is the house of the farmer who has charge of it, just as we know that the palace of the Procurator Cornaro was near the convent, and that nearer still was the house of his steward

In the Benvenuti garden there is running water, which is very scarce in these hills; this is made to pass through lead pipes. In fact, we find recorded in the inventory "eighty-six pipes of lead, weighing 2080 lbs ," to be used for the fountains. And, furthermore, a historian of Este, in 1743, published the following. "There is Cavalier Farsetti's villa near the convent of the Capuchins, where the house, being an unpretentious one, does not arouse great curiosity to see it; but the site and the playing fountains are worthy to be considered. and the place has frequent visitors." If we also examine minutely the engravings of Coronelli we shall see a portico of seven arches under the palace, in the garden a large stairway, with many flower vases on pedestals on each side; and, close by, two vine trellises The inventory, furthermore, mentions a portico below in the front of the palace, a stairway on the outside, numerous boxes and vases of plants—among them lemon trees, orange trees, and prickly-pear trees; fifty pedestals of stone for the orange trees, and vine trellises supported by columns of stone, connected by iron arches

These comparisons are more than sufficient to establish the identity of the two villas But, in ending, I shall not omit to add another piece of information furnished by the inventory In it is a full list of an interesting collection of pictures which were distributed about the rooms of the palace. Among them, besides "a Cornaro coat of arms painted on canvas," and a portrait of the well-known Queen of Cyprus, there is a painting of Ruzzante, the protégé and affectionate friend of Louis Cornaro, who used to frequent with him these lovely hills, and who, after the hunting, would recite in the hall which Cornaro had built in his own house Of this hall there is now no vestige; and the palace is really no longer the one of yore, as the architect of the Caffè Pedrocchi has repaired it on an extensive scale But Coronelli's engraving remains, and it gives us some idea of the physiognomy of the building erected by the famous author of "The Temperate Life."

We can suppose the same about the garden, on comparing the other engraving, where we see the stairway leading from the courtyard to the first floor of the palace, but not the classical archway which stood at the foot of it And yet the engraver Sebastiano Giampiccoli did not omit to picture it—though very imperfectly—with the garden and stairway, the palace and the large lateral conservatories, as did also an amateur, who, in 1775, engraved a panorama of the city We find it more faithfully reproduced in the "Design of the Ancient City of Este," of 1566, which accompanies the unpublished history of Michele Lonigo, to be found in the Estense Library of Modena This drawing proves that the

archway was there at least as early as the year following
Louis Cornaro's death, and it is reasonable to suppose that it
was he who built it, this supposition is strengthened by the
proofs of the great resemblance between the architectural
style of this arch and the works of Cornaro and his friend
Falconetto

The Este archway belongs to the Roman style, of which
the two were such enthusiastic admirers, and it is, indeed, a
free imitation of the archway of Janus Quadrifrons, erected
in Rome not earlier than the reign of Caracalla, or that of
Septimius Severus, or, according to some, as late as the time
of Constantine In the treatises on architecture of the sixteenth century it had already taken its place among the
models Furthermore, the two architects, Cornaro and Falconetto, must certainly have seen and examined it, during
their visits to Rome to study the building art of the ancients

In the modern, as well as in the ancient arch, there are
small niches, with vaultings in the shape of shells; but in the
former their number was reduced from twelve to eight in the
first two divisions, and were omitted altogether in the third
to the summit of the arch, on which there was simply an attic,
as on others of Falconetto's arches—but without inscriptions
or figures. The style of the little pillars between the niches
is not varied as in the Roman model; but only the Composite
is used, which was also called Triumphal, from the triumphal
archways. The grand arch itself rests on two protruding sills,
the keystone is sculptured, and the panaches are ornamented
by two flying Victories with their torches extended These
particulars, which are wanting in the arch of Janus, are found
in the works of Falconetto and the buildings erected by
Cornaro. In fact, the jambs of the famous portico present the
same shape as the archway—fine or heavy, as the case may
be Besides, the central arch of the portico bears two sculptured Goddesses of Fame, undoubtedly different and better,
but respectively analogous in the attitude of the arms; and the
next two parts of the archways inclose here, likewise, a head
of a satyr with ram's horns—an ornament used by the
Veronese artist also on the exterior of the gate of Savonarola

[206]

One could find other analogies beyond these, of which there is, perhaps, no need. Let us observe, instead, a difference which seems to contradict. The proportion between the width and the height of the opening in the Este archway is less than one-half, Falconetto, instead, always made the breadth surpass half of the height. But we must know here that, as Japelli had to lower the level of the court-yard, he lowered also the ground under the arch and lengthened the ends of the pillars, as is told us by the people of the place, and as is visible by the difference in the new stone which was used. To him, therefore, is due the alteration; and it does not in the least weaken the supposition that it was erected by Cornaro, perhaps with Falconetto's aid

Though my effort to arrive at this conclusion may, after all, appear to some a useless one, surely it will not be judged so by those who reflect that I have called the attention of the learned to a fine work of the closing period of the Venetian Renaissance—one which no one had as yet brought to notice.

Emilio Lovarini.

This is the excellent foppery of the world, that when we are sick in fortune—often the surfeit of our own behavior—we make guilty of our disasters the sun, the moon, and the stars· as if we were villains by necessity, fools by heavenly compulsion, knaves, thieves, and treachers, by spherical predominance, drunkards, liars, and adulterers, by an enforced obedience of planetary influence, and all that we are evil in, by a divine thrusting on an admirable evasion of man, to lay his goatish disposition to the charge of a star¹—"King Lear"

NOTES

A—According to the official count of the returns of the Twelfth Census, (Census Reports, Vol II, pp XXXVI. and XXXVIII), the population of the mainland of the United States (excluding Alaska, Hawaii, and persons in the military and naval service of the United States, stationed abroad) was, in 1900, as follows

Total	Males	Females
75,994,575	38,816,448 (51 1 per cent)	37,178,127 (48 9 per cent)

The number of persons returned as 90 years of age and over was 33,762, classified by sex and age groups as follows

	Total	Men	Per cent	Women	Per cent
90 to 94 years	23,992	9,858	41 1	14,134	58 9
95 to 99 years	6,266	2,417	38 6	3,849	61 4
100 years and over	3,504	1,271	36 3	2,233	63 7

B—John Witt Randall (1813—1892) was a great-grandson of Samuel Adams, the American Revolutionary patriot This poem was selected by William Cullen Bryant for publication in his review of Randall's "Consolations of Solitude" The article appeared in the New York "Evening Post" of December 17, 1856 The poem is here reproduced by courtesy of Francis Ellingwood Abbot, editor of Randall's "Poems of Nature and Life" (George H Ellis, Boston 1899)

C—In the selections from Addison, Bacon, Temple, etc , the spelling and punctuation have been, to some extent modernized The Bacon article is not an unbroken section of his works, but a collection of many short passages, in the arrangement of which we have avoided the use of the customary indication of omissions of irrelevant matter The same is true of the article from Temple's works

The given name of the author of "The Temperate Life" has long been familiar to his English readers in its anglicized form, and we have thought it best, in speaking of the members of his family, to insert the English equivalents of their names, where such exist, with the object of bringing the work as near as possible to the general reader

D—The Di Spilimbergo family was an Italian patrician branch of a house of German origin, which, as early as the 13th century, resided and ruled in that part of Friuli, in northern Italy, known as Spilim-bergo This noble and ancient house was very powerful, exercising—

in some cases feudal, in others allodial—lordship over many vast estates, among which were the castles of Spilimbergo, Zuccola, Solimbergo, Flambro, Belgrado, and others The family, ennobled in 1532 by Emperor Charles V, numbered among its eminent members many soldiers, statesmen, prelates, and artists—one of the latter being the famous painter, Irene di Spilimbergo (1540-1559) The city of Spilimbergo,—of which the population in 1901 was 2,331,—on the Tajamento, 14 miles west of Udine, was named after this family

E—**Giovanni Maria** (John Mary) **Falconetto,** one of the most eminent of Italian architects, was born at Verona, in 1458 He studied architecture at Rome, then returned to Verona, later making his home in Padua Greatly improving the style of architecture in the Venetian states, he designed and constructed many admirable buildings and other works in Padua, Verona, and elsewhere His masterpiece, the celebrated Cornaro Loggia in Padua, suggested to Palladio the design of his villa at Vicenza, the famous Rotonda Capra; the latter—once one of the greatest monuments of modern architectural art, and described by Goethe as a marvel of splendor—has, in its turn, served as a copy for others, among them the beautiful Chiswick House, the villa of the dukes of Devonshire, at Chiswick, England In the Church of San Antonio, in Padua, the Cappella del Santo, so remarkable for its grandeur and beauty, was completed by him. He died in 1534

F—**Claudius Galenus,** commonly known as Galen, the most eminent physician, as well as one of the most learned and accomplished men, of his day, was born at Pergamus, in Mysia, Asia Minor, A. D. 130 At the age of fifteen he studied logic and philosophy at his native city, two years later he began the study of medicine, continuing it at Smyrna, Corinth, and Alexandria At the age of thirty-four he removed to Rome, there he gained great fame, and became the physician of the illustrious philosopher, Emperor Marcus Aurelius Antoninus, as well as of the Emperors Lucius Verus, Lucius Aurelius Commodus, and Lucius Septimius Severus He was born with a very delicate constitution; yet, by living a strictly temperate life and never fully satisfying his appetite, he was enabled to attain great age The place and date of his death are uncertain, occurring, according to some historians, at his native city, in the year 201, while others place the date as much as eighteen years later There are good reasons for believing the latter to be correct

Galen confessed himself greatly indebted to the writings of Hippocrates, who preceded him about six centuries, and who is known as The Father of Medicine. He was an extensive writer on medicine and philosophy, as well as on logic and ethics; of his works there are still in existence eighty-three treatises, besides fifteen commentaries on the works of Hippocrates. For thirteen hundred years, throughout Europe and the East, Galen was the recognized authority in the science of medicine.

G—Doge (the Venetian modified form of the Italian duce, from the Latin dux, a leader or duke) was the title of the chief magistrate of the Republic of Venice The dignity, or office, was called Dogato. The incumbent was always elected for life, and was originally chosen by universal suffrage He continued to acquire more and more irresponsible authority, until, in 1033 and 1172, laws were passed which, in various ways, greatly reduced his power These included the association with him of a body of 470 councilors, known as the Great Council At the same time universal suffrage was abolished

In 1268, the doge—"King in the forum, senator in the legislative hall, prisoner in the palace"—was elected by a peculiarly complex method, which remained in vogue, with but little change, until the fall of the Republic· thirty members of the Great Council, elected by ballot, chose nine members, they, in their turn, chose forty; twelve of these forty, selected by lot, chose twenty-five, the twenty-five were reduced to nine, the nine elected forty-five; the forty-five were reduced to eleven, and the eleven chose the final forty-one, in whose hands lay the actual election of the doge The powers of the doge became, in time, so restricted as to be little more than nominal; and the constant espionage to which he was subjected, made the office less sought for than in the past, indeed, in 1339, it was necessary to forbid, by law, the resignation of the incumbent There were, in all, one hundred and twenty doges, the first, Paolo Lucio Anafesto, was elected in 697, the last, Lodovico Manin, in 1789 Of the whole number, the Cornaro family furnished four

H—After the dignity of Doge, that of Procurator of St. Mark (Italian, Procuratore di San Marco) was the highest Originally, there was only one procurator, but, in 1442, the number was increased to nine They discharged functions of a varied and responsible character, and were designated as follows the procurator de supra (above), in whose care was the imposing Basilica of St Mark—one of the most interesting churches in Europe, begun in 828 but not consecrated until 1111—as well as the revenues attached to it, the procurator de citra (this side), who had charge of the charitable works on "this side", and the procurator de ultra (beyond), who had charge of them on "that side,"—of the Grand Canal As the office was bestowed only upon the foremost men of the day, it was occupied by many whose names form a part of Venetian, and often of European, history Twenty-two members of the Cornaro family are found in this roll of illustrious men, which ended with the fall of the Republic

I—The Euganean Hills (Italian, Colli Euganei) were so named from the people, who, according to Livy, occupied this territory until

driven out by the Veneti   The highest point is Monte Venda   These
hills are covered with a luxuriant growth, and the views from their
summits are the finest in all Italy   It was the red larch, and the
granitic and porphyritic rocks abounding there, that were largely used
in the construction of the Doge's Palace—built originally about the
year 820—and other famous buildings of Venice   Of the many col-
lections of prehistoric relics found in these hills, that in the Museum
of Antiquities of Mantua is especially interesting and valuable   With
lovers of musical verse, Shelley's poem, "Lines Written Among the
Euganean Hills" has long been a familiar favorite

J—Danielle (Daniel) Barbaro, an Italian ecclesiastic and Patriarch of Aquileia, was born at Venice, in 1513   He was an extensive
writer, among his works being a treatise, "On Eloquence," and a com-
mentary, "On the Architecture of Vitruvius", the latter contributing
largely toward the return to the classical style of architecture.   His
beautiful residence, a unique specimen of the villas of the Venetian
nobility of the period, was created and adorned by the united genius
of three of the great artists of the Renaissance —Andrea Palladio,
Paolo Veronese and Allessandro Vittoria,—and was a noted center of
arts and letters   He died in 1570

K—Aquileia, an ancient city at the head of the Adriatic, 22 miles
northwest of Trieste, was colonized by the Romans about 181 B C
At a later period it was chosen by Julius Cæsar as headquarters for
his forces in Cisalpine Gaul   In 160, the Emperor Marcus Aurelius
Antoninus fortified it so strongly that it was considered the first
bulwark of the Roman Empire against the northern barbarians, and
was called The Second Rome   At one time it was the capital and
first city of Venetia   In the 5th century it had 100,000 inhabitants,
but, in 452, it was destroyed by Attila, King of the Huns, and the
inhabitants fled to the lagoons on which Venice now stands   From
this it never fully recovered, yet, rebuilt, it continued to enjoy considerable prosperity   At the council of 556, the Bishop of Aquileia
separated from the Church of Rome and took the title of Patriarch
In 1420, Venice deprived it of most of its possessions, and, in the
latter half of the eighteenth century, the Patriarchate was abolished
The city is said to have derived its name from the Latin aquila, an
eagle having appeared as a favorable omen to its founders, but it is
more probable that the name owes its origin to the fact that the
"aquila" was the standard of the Romans   The population is now
about 2,000

L—The Cornelii ranked among the most illustrious of the patrician families of Rome, and no other house produced a greater number
of individuals who notably distinguished themselves in war and
civil affairs   To this family belonged Cornelia,—daughter of the
famous Scipio, and wife of Tiberius Sempronius Gracchus,—who is

known in history not only as Cornelia, Mother of the Gracchi, but also as the purest woman mentioned in the historical period of Rome She was the mother of twelve children and lived to extreme old age, dying about 130 B C

M—The **Bucentaur** (Italian, Il Bucentoro), the state galley of the Venetian doges, was employed to conduct illustrious guests, whom the Republic delighted to honor, to the Ducal Palace. It was also used in the ceremony of espousing the Adriatic, into whose waters the doge dropped a ring, with these words "We espouse thee, Sea, in token of true and perpetual sovereignty" This historic custom, which was in itself a proclamation and a challenge to the world, originated in the celebration of the triumph, in 1177, of the Venetians under Sebastiano Ziani, the 39th doge, over the forces of Frederick I (Barbarossa), Emperor of Germany, and was annually observed, without interruption and with all its original pomp and splendor, from that year until the close of the Republic in 1797 The galley, 100 feet long and 21 feet in extreme breadth was manned by 168 rowers, four to each oar, and by 40 sailors Its fittings, gorgeous in the extreme, were brilliant with scarlet and gold, its long banks of oars brightly burnished, and its deck and seats inlaid with costly woods The ship perhaps received its name from the figure of a bucentaur—head of a man and body of a bull—in the bow.

N—**The Golden Book** (Italian, Il Libro d'Oro), was the parchment register in which were kept the complete records of the births, marriages, deaths etc, of all the members of the Venetian hereditary nobility. Anyone enrolled in this famous register, had he attained the age of twenty-five and been found worthy, was eligible to membership in the Great Council It was a unique institution, opened in 1315, it enjoyed a duration of centuries, until it was closed, forever, in the fatal year of 1797 It is now among the archives of the Republic

O—Bartolomeo (Bartholomew) **Gamba,** a noted Italian biographer and author, was born at Bassano —on the river Brenta, in northern Italy,—May 15, 1766 As a distinguished printer and editor, he was elected, in 1831, Vice-Librarian of the Marciana There he acquired such fame as a bibliographer, that he was made a member of several Italian academies, including the one at Florence Among his many writings, acknowledged to be of great merit, are "A Gallery of the Literati and Artists of the Venetian Provinces in the Eighteenth Century" (1824), and his "Life of Dante" (1825) He died May 3, 1841

P—**Caius Cilnius Mæcenas,** a celebrated Roman statesman, and the most influential patron of literature at Rome, was born about 70 B C, of an ancient and noble Etruscan family He was, for many years, the intimate friend, as well as chief minister and adviser, of

[213]

THE ART OF LIVING LONG

the Emperor Augustus, by whom he was held in the highest respect and honor. His palace, on the Esquiline Hill, was long the principal resort of the literati of Rome. It was chiefly due to his aid that the poets Horace and Virgil were granted the means for the enjoyment of literary leisure, and the latter wrote his "Georgics" at the request of his benefactor. His death, occurring at Rome, in the year 8 B. C., was considered by all—especially by Augustus—an irreparable loss. As early as the 1st century his name had become proverbial as a patron of letters; indeed, among all the names—royal, noble, or otherwise eminent—associated with their patronage, none in ancient or modern times is so familiarly known as that of Mæcenas, a century after whose death the poet Martial wrote: "Let there but be Mæcenases, and Virgils shall not be lacking." Mæcenas is a familiar character in Shakespeare's "Antony and Cleopatra."

Q—**Ruzzante,** a favorite Italian dramatic poet, whose true name was Angelo Beolco, was born at Padua, in 1502. Gifted with remarkable talent, he was the author of many dialogues, discourses, and various other writings in the rustic Paduan dialect, which he had thoroughly mastered. The large number of comedies which he composed were all highly applauded wherever heard.

A few young men of good family accompanied him on his travels as an artist, reciting, as he did, under the shelter of a disguise—concealing their real names under others borrowed from the scenes in which they appeared. In the recital of these farces he took the part of the joker or jester (Italian, Ruzzante); and it was to this circumstance that he owed his sobriquet of Ruzzante, which clung to him ever after. Indeed, from that time on, he used it instead of his family name; it even appeared in his works, which were published, complete, at Vicenza, in 1584, 1598, and 1617, under the title: "All the Works of the Most Famous Ruzzante, Newly and with the Greatest Diligence Revised and Corrected." He died March 17, 1542.

R—**Emilio Lorenzo Lovarini,** professor of Italian literature in the royal Liceo (High School) Minghetti, of Bologna, was born at Venice, March 7, 1866. His youth was passed in Padua, where he completed his education, receiving his degree of doctor of philology from the University of that city, July, 1889.

Although still a young man, Dr. Lovarini has already acquired considerable reputation as an authority on various subjects, his researches covering a wide range. His chief writings pertain to the customs, dialect, folk lore, and rustic literature of ancient Padua; the habits and pastimes of students of the University in the 16th century, etc. He is the author, also, of a biography of Ruzzante, an illustrated critical edition of whose works he is now preparing. He has published a highly interesting work on gypsy melodies, and the songs of Taranto

[214]

WETZEL BROS.
PRINTING COMPANY,
MILWAUKEE

CPSIA information can be obtained at www.ICGtesting.com
Printed in the USA
LVOW131143210212

269702LV00012B/88/P

9 781172 084449